Gardening in Arabia

Ornamental Trees in Qatar and the Arabian Gulf

Gardening in Arabia: Ornamental Trees in Qatar and the Arabian Gulf.

First published in 2018 by Hamad Bin Khalifa University Press.
P O Box 5825
Doha, Qatar
www.hbkupress.com

Copyright © 2018 by Shuaa Abdullah Hussain Al-Sada.
www.gardeninginarabia.com

The moral right of the author has been asserted.

Some of the facts set forth in this work are not those of the author and do not necessarily reflect her views. She cannot be held responsible for them.

No part of this book and no picture in it may be reproduced in any way without written permission from the author. Every reasonable effort has been made to trace copyright holders of material reproduced in this book, but if any have been inadvertently overlooked the publishers would be glad to hear from them.

ISBN: 9789927129230

Printed in China by Everbest.

Front cover
Hibiscus tiliaceus
Sea hibiscus flower

Back cover
Thespesia populnea
Umbrella tree flower

Right
Cassia fistula
Golden shower tree buds

Gardening in Arabia

Ornamental Trees in Qatar and the Arabian Gulf

Shuaa Abdullah Al-Sada

CONSULTANTS: Sabina Knees and Lorna MacKinnon

CONSULTANCY

Astronomy consultant
Salman Jabor Althani
Qatar Astronomical Center

Horticultural and
botanical consultants
Dr Sabina Knees
and Lorna MacKinnon

Linxian Wang
Sr. Landscape Architect

ARTWORK/DESIGN

Photography
Natalie Gueris
Linxian Wang
Herbert Villadelrey

Contributing photographers
Moudhi Alhajiri
Larry Issa
Zaki Jamil

Design
Larry Issa
LMI Design

Digital artist
2AM

Map
Martin Lubikowski
ML Design, London

EDITORIAL

Editors
Margie Rae Jackson
Taiba Saoud Al-Rodaini
Michelle Wallin

Above left to right
Moringa oleifera
Miracle tree flower;
Plumeria
Frangipani flowers;
Leucaena leucocephala
White leadtree flower

Opposite page
Parkinsonia aculeata
Jerusalem thorn flowers

*In the Name of Allah,
The Most Gracious,
The Most Merciful*

I would like to thank everyone who has helped and encouraged me during the writing of this book, especially my husband for his moral and financial support, and my children, who have been extremely patient and understanding during my many hours of work. I would also like to thank Baba Mohammad, my gardener for over 15 years, for sharing his knowledge and experience of gardening in the Arabian Gulf region; my neighbor Sarah Al-Naimi, for welcoming me into her garden and allowing me to photograph her plants; and Asma Al-Kabi, for her invaluable contacts and knowledge of where to find things in Qatar. A special thanks to Natalie Gueris, my friend, photographer, and fellow adventurer, as well as Linxian Wang, Moudhi Alhajiri, and Herbert Villadelrey, for the stunning photographs they have taken for this book. Thanks to Margie Rae Jackson, for her help with editing the English text; to Larry Issa, for his work on the book's layout and also for driving this project forward; and to the many others who contributed in one way or another. Particular thanks to those who allowed us to take photographs at their venues, especially, Plaza Hollandi, and Grand Hyatt Doha, especially Mohamed Taha Mahmoud Moustafa.

Left
Senna surattensis
Golden senna flowers

Contents

- 1 Introduction
- 3 Climate of the Arabian Gulf region
- 5 Gardening by the Arabian stars
- 11 Perennials
- 13 Plant physiology
- 15 Trees
  - 17 Introduction to trees
  - 23 *Acacia*, Wattle
  - 37 *Adansonia digitata*, African Baobab Tree
  - 43 *Albizia*, Silk Tree
  - 47 *Azadirachta indica*, Neem Tree
  - 51 *Bambusa*, Bamboo
  - 55 *Bauhinia*, Orchid Tree
  - 61 *Boswellia sacra*, Frankincense
  - 65 *Bucida molineti*, Spiny Black Olive
  - 67 *Butea monosperma*, Flame of the Forest
  - 73 *Callistemon viminalis*, Weeping Bottlebrush
  - 77 *Cascabela thevetia*, Yellow Oleander
  - 81 *Cassia*, Cassia Tree
  - 87 *Casuarina equisetifolia*, Horsetail Tree
  - 91 *Ceiba*, Silk Cotton Tree
  - 97 *Cerbera manghas*, Sea Mango
  - 101 *Coccoloba uvifera*, Sea Grape
  - 105 *Cochlospermum religiosum*, Buttercup Tree
  - 109 *Conocarpus lancifolius*, Damas Tree
  - 113 *Cordia*, Orange/White Cordia
  - 117 *Cupressus*, Cypress
  - 121 *Dalbergia sissoo*, Indian Rosewood
  - 125 *Delonix regia*, Royal Poinciana
  - 131 *Erythrina*, Coral Tree

137	*Eucalyptus,* Gum Tree, Ironbark Tree	273	Palms
141	*Ficus,* Ficus Tree	275	Introduction to palms
151	*Gliricidia sepium,* Mexican Lilac	279	*Acoelorrhaphe wrightii,* Saw Palm
155	*Handroanthus chrysanthus,* Golden Trumpet	283	*Bismarckia nobilis,* Silver Frond Palm
157	*Hibiscus tiliaceus,* Sea Hibiscus	287	*Caryota mitis,* Burmese Fishtail Palm
161	*Jacaranda mimosifolia,* Blue Jacaranda	291	*Chamaerops humilis,* Dwarf Fan Palm
165	*Kigelia africana,* Sausage Tree	293	*Copernicia alba,* Caranday Palm, Wax Palm
169	*Lagerstroemia,* Crepe Myrtle, Pride of India	297	*Dypsis decaryi,* Triangle Palm
175	*Lawsonia inermis,* Henna Tree	301	*Elaeis guineensis,* African Oil Palm
179	*Leucaena leucocephala,* White Leadtree	305	*Hyphaene thebaica,* Doum Palm
183	*Melia azedarach,* Chinaberry	309	*Licuala grandis,* Ruffled Fan Palm
187	*Millingtonia hortensis,* Tree Jasmine	311	*Livistona chinensis,* Chinese Fan Palm
191	*Mimusops elengi,* Spanish Cherry	315	*Phoenix,* Palmae
195	*Moringa,* Miracle Tree, Ben Tree	325	*Ravenala madagascariensis,* Traveller's Palm
203	*Parkinsonia aculeata,* Jerusalem Thorn	329	*Rhapis excelsa,* Broadleaf Lady Palm
207	*Peltophorum pterocarpum,* Yellow Flame Tree	333	*Roystonea regia,* Royal Palm
211	*Platycladus orientalis,* Oriental Thuja	337	*Sabal palmetto,* Cabbage Palm
215	*Plumeria,* Frangipani	341	*Washingtonia,* Desert Fan
221	*Polyalthia longifolia,* False Ashoka Tree	345	*Wodyetia bifurcata,* Foxtail Palm
225	*Pongamia pinnata,* Poona Oil Tree	348	References
229	*Prosopis,* Ghaf Tree, Mesquite	350	Glossary
233	*Schinus,* Pepper Tree		
237	*Senna,* Golden Senna, Empress Candle		
243	*Spathodea campanulata,* African Tulip Tree		
247	*Tabebuia,* Trumpet Tree		
253	*Tamarix aphyll*a, Athel Tree		
257	*Tecoma stans,* Yellow Bells		
261	*Tecomella undulata,* Desert Teak		
265	*Thespesia populnea,* Umbrella Tree		
269	*Vitex agnus-castus,* Chaste Tree		

Opposite page
Jacaranda mimosifolia
Blue jacaranda flowers

Introduction

The Messenger of Allah, peace and blessings be upon him, said, "There is no Muslim who plants a tree or sows seeds and then a bird, or a person, or an animal eats from it except that it is charity for him."

I thank God who provides us with all that we need in this world, especially the plants and flowers that nourish us both physically and spiritually and bring us such happiness. Plants create islands of peace and serenity amidst the stress and commotion of our daily lives. They require only water, soil, and sun; in return they offer beauty, nourishment, and healing. Planting a garden can instil hope and joy, even provide meaning to life where there was none. Cultivating a garden generates a thousand and one things to look forward to: the day a flower will open, a tree will grow, or a fruit will ripen.

When I started writing this series of books I did it with the intention of helping to guide anyone with a similar passion for plants to identify them easily, understand how they grow and realize the benefits of each plant. However, my main purpose is not limited to promoting knowledge of plants; it is also to inspire and encourage every home to have a garden. Gardening is easy and, with a little effort, anyone can achieve a beautiful and bountiful garden, a private oasis of tranquility and harmony for the family. Aside from being a wonderful activity that the whole household can contribute to and benefit from, gardening also helps to protect our environment by increasing the amount of greenery.

For all of these reasons, among others, I wish to invite you, dear readers, to create your own garden, whether indoors or outdoors. I think you will be pleasantly surprised at the wide variety of plants that can be grown in your garden, despite our country's semi-desert conditions of high temperatures, little rain, and poor soil. During the growing season, from October to April, all types of plants can thrive. By nourishing the soil with vitamins and fertilizer, and providing care and attention, we can all make our gardens beautiful.

Shuaa Abdullah Al-Sada

Opposite page
Bauhinia
Orchid tree flower

Climate of the Arabian Gulf region

The Arabian Gulf region comprises seven countries, namely: Bahrain, Iraq, Kuwait, Oman, Qatar, Saudi Arabia and the United Arab Emirates. While these countries all border the Arabian Gulf, they span a vast and varied geographical area and display a large range of climate types, from hot and dry desert regions to high mountainous areas that have cold spells. Temperatures across the Gulf exhibit significant regional and seasonal fluctuations, ranging from extreme winter lows of -5°C to 0°C in the higher elevations of Saudi Arabia and Oman, to scorching summer highs of 42°C to 52°C in the deserts of Bahrain, Kuwait, Qatar and Saudi Arabia. Humidity fluctuates regionally and seasonally, ranging from between 35% to 70% in winter, and from 15% to as much as 90% in summer. Average rainfall for the Arabian Gulf is about 152mm a year, occurring almost exclusively during the winter months. Precipitation also varies widely across the region, however, with some areas averaging as little as 30mm a year, and others as much as 435mm. Countries with little average rainfall often depend on desalinated water for irrigation.

Gardening by the Arabian stars

January
Important dates—2nd: Two small stars, one larger than the other, rise together in a configuration that farmers call *al-Marbaaneah*. They are present in the night sky for 13 days, and during this time the weather is seasonably cold.

—15th: The constellation of *al-Naaim*, which farmers call *al-Shabat al-Awaal*, ascends. This is the fourth of the winter constellations, appearing between Scorpius and Sagittarius, and will remain in the sky for 13 days. While this cluster of stars, also known as *Enkood al-Farasha*, rises during a period of severe cold, by the time the cluster begins its descent new leaves will start to emerge on trees. These stars are sometimes called *bil Naaim*, because at this time if it is cold enough the plants in the desert become very green; however, if temperatures fall too low small plants in the desert will burn from the cold. Planting during this time is not recommended, as the groundwater may be frozen and will not be available to nurture plant roots. Around this time the leaves of the *Erythina caffra* and neem trees begin to fall.

—21st: This is the first day of the zodiac sign Aquarius, the second sign of the winter season. Aquarius lasts for 30 days, and during this time temperatures rise and groundwater melts, once again nourishing the roots of plants. This is a good time to relocate or replant small date palms and other saplings.

—28th: This date ushers in the cluster called *al-Balda*, considered to be the fifth constellation of winter. It consists of six small, dim stars that are seen with difficulty by the naked eye. Mature trees such as *Millingtonia hortensis* and *Tabebuia rosea*, begin to flower.

February
Important dates—10th: This date marks the appearance of taleh *Saad al-Dabeh* (Beta Capricorni, Dabih), which consists of two stars, one very bright and the other comparatively dim. The first can be found high in the northern side of the sky while the other is low in the south. These stars become visible by the end of winter.

—20th: This date marks the beginning of the time of Pisces, the last constellation in the Arabian calendar. This phase consists of 29–30 days.

—23rd: Two stars ascend at this time, together called *Saad Albali*. They are said to herald rain, which helps plants to flourish and last longer come spring.

Gardening: This is the time to start planting for spring. All tree types are available in nurseries. *Conocarpus lancifolius* can be propagated using cuttings from existing specimens.

March
Important dates—8th: This marks the appearance of *taleh Salsuud* (Beta Aquarii, Sadalsuud), consisting of three stars, one which shines very brightly and two which are very dim. They bring with them the change to more clement weather and, with this shift, plants begin to flourish. New leaves emerge on *Vitex agnus-castus* trees.

*Taleh can be approximately described as 'ascension' in an astronomical sense; it forms part of the traditional Arab calendar wherein celestial bodies are tracked to herald propitious cycles for such human activities as farming and animal breeding.

Opposite page
Plumeria
Frangipani flowers

—21st: This marks the beginning Aries, whose length is 31 days, and the first stars of spring. The constellation *Saad al-Akhbeeya* ascends and is visible for 13 days. This cluster consists of four stars, all very close together. As the month comes to an end, days and nights start to become equal in length. Neem trees begin to flower.

Gardening: Spring is in the air; trees are flowering and starting to produce fruit. At this time *Azadirachta indica*, *Causarina equestifolia*, *Cochlospermum religiosum*, *Erythrina variegata*, *Tabebuia rosea*, *Tabebuia argentea*, and many other trees are in bloom. This is the perfect time to start planting all types of seeds, seedlings and saplings.

April
Important dates—3rd: The two stars of *taleh al-Mokadam* (*Marchab* and *Manib al-Faras*) become visible. Farmers call this constellation *al-Hameem al-Thani*. It lasts for 13 days. This also marks the beginning of the pollen season, which in some people can cause allergic reactions, including rhinitis, hay fever and asthma. Due to the pollen, the consumption of salted fish should be avoided during this time.

—16th: This marks the appearance of *taleh al-Mu'akhir* (Alpha Andromedae, Sirrah and Gamma Pegasi), which is also called *Ziraa' al-Awal* ("first forearm") by farmers. These two stars are visible for 13 days, and are part of the constellation *al-Mara'ah al-Musalsalah* (The Shackled Woman). *Delonix regia* will lose their leaves, and *Hibiscus tilliaceus* will come into flower.

—21st: The constellation *al-Thawr* (Taurus) appears, which is the second constellation of spring. During this time, all kinds of seeds are sown. Pay extra attention to irrigation, especially for small plants, as the hot summer starts soon.

—29th: Two stars, *al-Rasha* (Upsilon Piscium and Phi Piscium), appear in the abdomen of the Pisces constellation. Farmers call this time *Airaa' Athani* ("second forearm"). Strong winds arrive, commonly known in Gulf Arabic as *Riyah al-Meshmesh* ("the peach winds"). In some countries of the region, they are accompanied by heavy rain.

Gardening: All kinds of trees begin to flower, and fruit trees and seeds for summer plants can be sown. At this time *Cassia fistula* and *Gliricidia sepium* are in full bloom.

May
Important dates—12th: The constellation *al-Shartin* (Beta Arietis, Gamma Arietis) becomes visible, bringing with it fair weather in many parts of the world, with the exception of the Arabian Gulf, where seasonal flowers begin to fade.

—22nd: This date marks the advent of the North wind, which grows in intensity to reach maximum strength around the 25th of May.

—25th: *Taleh al-Bateen*, which farmers call *Thoraya al-Kaiith*, ascends on this date, and will be visible for 13 days. This cluster consists of three dim stars that are part of the Aries constellation. Strong North winds continue to dominate the weather at this time.

Gardening: Most flowering trees, including *Prosopis cineraria* and *Vitex agnus-castus*, are in bloom, and some trees, such as *Cochlospermum religiosum*, are bearing fruit. Many palm trees are also flowering, including *Washingtonia filifera*, *Phoenix dactylifera*, and *Phoenix roebelenii*.

June
Important dates—7th: *Taleh al-Thuraya* (Pleiades, M45) ascends, consisting of the cluster known as the Seven Sisters. This set of stars resembles a question mark, and is clearly visible in the night sky for 13 days. With the appearance of this cluster, the weather becomes dry and hot.

—20th: The appearance of the star Aldebaran in the Taurus constellation marks the three shortest nights of the year, after which nights gradually begin to grow in length. Farmers call this bright star *al-Tuwayb*, and it is visible for 13 days. Traditionally, people are advised not to eat beans or onions, or anything cold and soft, during this time.

—22nd: The rise of the constellation Cancer marks the beginning of summer. Traditionally, drinking cold beverages is advised at this time.

Gardening: Around the 20th of this month *Cordia sebestena* reaches its flowering peak, and the neem tree is in full bloom as well.

July
Important dates—3rd: This date marks the appearance of the three stars of *taleh al-Haka* (Lambda Orionis), which farmers call *Bil Jozaa al-Ula*. This cluster, which is visible for 13 days, heralds the start of the intensely hot weather across the Arabian Gulf region.

—16th: A pair of bright stars called *taleh al-Hanaa*, also known by farmers as *Bil Jozaa al-Thania*, rise into view. These two stars are part of a larger constellation called the Two Orphans, and they are visible for 13 days. During this time the weather is very hot, and the roots of trees stop growing.

—23rd: The sun moves into Leo, the second constellation of the summer. During this period, the intense heat is often accompanied by strong easterly and southeasterly sea winds that increase humidity levels. In previous generations in the Arabian Gulf region, particularly in Qatar, this was traditionally the time when pearls were harvested from the sea.

—29th: *Taleh al-Thuraa*, a cluster of stars from the Two Orphans constellation, ascends. These stars, known by farmers as *Bil Marrzam*, are visible for 13 days.

Gardening: Trees are producing fruit, and the fruits of the neem tree are ripening from green to yellow. Due to the extremely high temperatures, it is not advised to plant any seeds or seedlings at this time, and plants that are less tolerant of strong sunlight should be covered during the day.

August
Important dates—11th: This marks the appearance of *taleh al-Nathra* (Beehive Cluster, M44), which farmers call *Bil Kalibeen*. These stars, which are part of the larger constellation Cancer, are arranged like a cluster of grapes. They are visible for 13 days.

—23rd: Plants need to be watered very frequently and the soil must be worked so that it is ready for planting. This date sees the rise of the last constellation of summer, called *al-Sunbulah*.

—24th: Canopus, the second brightest star of the nighttime sky, rises over the Arabian Peninsula and the surrounding areas, including Jordan and the region known as *Bilad al-Sham* (the Levant), which contains modern-day Syria. In addition to Canopus, two stars, together known as *taleh al-Turfa*, ascend, defining the two eyes of the Leo constellation. They are visible for 13 days. The rise of these two stars marks a change of wind direction in Qatar. This change causes the clouds to pool together, and facilitates rain in the northwest part of the country. This precipitation is known as the rains before *al-Wasmi*, and although this rain does not water the ground enough to initiate plant growth, it does prepare the soil for the coming season.

Gardening: During this month plants are particularly prone to insects and pests.

September

Important dates—6th: The bright cluster *taleh al-Giebha* (Gamma Leonis, Algieba), also known to farmers as *b'al-Ashrut*, rises. These four stars, located in the mane of the Leo constellation, reside in the sky for 14 days. It occasionally rains at this time in some areas of the Arabian Gulf region, which is very beneficial to planting.

—20th: This marks the appearance of the vivid cluster *al-Zubra* (Delta Leonis, Duhr), located on the hip of the Leo constellation. Also known by farmers as *al-Hurrthan*, these two stars, one brighter than the other, will remain visible for 13 days. While nights become cooler, daytime temperatures remain high, and are rendered more intense by the seasonal northern winds. It rarely rains at this time.

—23rd: The constellation Libra, the first constellation of fall, ascends. It will remain visible for 30 days. While days and nights are still relatively equal in length, nights are gradually becoming longer, marking the beginning of autumn.

Gardening: Towards the end of September *Millingtonia hortensis* is flowering and *Chamaerops humilis* will begin to produce fruit. All types of palm trees can be found in local nurseries.

October

Important dates—3rd: This marks the appearance of *taleh al-Surfa* (Beta Leonis, Denebola), known by farmers as *Akhr Najoom Suhail*. Visible for 13 days, this is the third of the autumn constellations. Consisting of one bright star, located on the tail of the Leo constellation, and several dimmer stars, this cluster is also called *al-Surfa*. In Arabic *al-surfa* means "to go", and this is the time of the year when the hot weather finally goes away. The weather begins to cool and it is around this time that the rains start, commonly known in Gulf Arabic as *al-Wasmi*. These rains are very important to the region because they herald the growth of Gulf truffles; if the rains do not arrive, the truffles will not appear. The coming of *al-Wasmi* is a cause for thanksgiving and celebration throughout the Gulf.

—16th: *Taleh al-Owa*, also known by farmers as *Thoraya al-Wasmi*, ascends. This cluster, consisting of stars from the Virgo constellation, is visible in the sky for 13 days. At this time it is traditionally ill-advised to eat cold items, beef, or eggplant.

—29th: Heavy rains start with the rising of *taleh al-Samaak* (Alpha Virginis, Spica). Farmers call this pair of stars *Tuwayba al-Wasmi*, and it is the second constellation of the *al-Wasmi* season. These two stars are located in the leg of the lion Leo. While in the past the rains at this time were so severe they would cause floods, in recent years the weather has not been as disruptive.

Gardening: October is the most important planting month in the Arabian Gulf region. Around the 16th of this month is the optimum time to plant all kinds of trees, shrubs, and climbers, annuals or perennials. This is the time to plant seeds for crops, and also to propagate trees by grafting. In the garden, *Ceiba speciosa* begins flowering. Tasks to be completed this month include propagation of *Conocarpus lancifolius*.

November
Important dates—11th: This date marks the appearance of *taleh al-Qafar* (Iota Virginis, Syrma), which farmers call *Jozaa al-Wasmi al-Ula*. This cluster, consisting of three slightly dim stars from the Virgo constellation, is visible at dawn for 13 days. It is the third constellation of the *al-Wasmi* season. At this time, *Bauhinia* trees are in full bloom.

—22nd: Orion, the last constellation of autumn, ascends as winter approaches.

—24th: This marks the appearance of Beta Librae (traditionally known as Zubeneschamali) and named *taleh al-Zabana*. It is in the constellation of Libra, the fourth constellation of the rainy *al-Wasmi* season. It consists of two stars, each from either scale in Libra. This time traditionally brings strong winds and heavy rains.

Gardening: Local nurseries are full of all kinds of plants during this month.

December
Important dates—7th: This marks the appearance of *taleh al-Eklil* (Beta Scorpii, Delta Scorpii, Pi Scorpii), which farmers call *al-Murrbaania Murrzim al-Raaee*. This cluster of three stars, delineating the head of the Scorpius constellation, is visible for 13 days. It does not always rain at this time; if it does rain, however, Gulf truffles will definitely grow in the desert.

—20th: At the heart of the Scorpius constellation is a shiny star called *al-Qalb* (Alpha Scorpii, Antares). Farmers know this star as *al-Ahaimir al-Murrbaania*, and it is visible for 13 days. The appearance of this star marks the beginning of winter.

—22nd: At this time the constellation Sagittarius takes its place in the night sky, remaining there for 30 days. This is the first constellation of winter, and with it comes long nights, short days, and very cold weather. *Vitex agnus-castus* trees will lose their leaves.

Gardening: While winter is a dormant season for plants in many parts of the world, it is an excellent time to work in the garden in Qatar.

Perennials

This plant group has a life cycle of more than two years, and includes plants such as trees, shrubs, climbers and woody-based perennials, as well as long-lived herbaceous species. While some perennials live only a few years, others have life spans of 100 years or more.

There are two types of perennials:

Evergreen perennials: In some species, perennials retain their foliage all year round. Examples of evergreen perennials include palm trees, palm-like trees, and conifers.

Deciduous perennials: This type of perennial loses its leaves during the dry season, or in the winter. An example of a deciduous perennial is the *Erythrina caffra* tree.

Opposite page
Tecomella undulata
Desert teak flowers

Above
Cordia sebestena
Orange cordia flowers

Plant physiology
Internal workings of plants and trees

God says in the Holy Quran: Surat Ibrahim, Verse 24:
Have you not considered how Allah presents an example, [making] a good word like a good tree, whose root is firmly fixed and its branches [high] in the sky?

To provide an environment where plants and trees can grow and thrive, it is necessary to understand the life processes of the plant. Trees absorb and transport food and water in the outer layers of their branches, trunk, and roots. If these layers become damaged or are removed, the tree will die. Transportation in these layers moves in both directions, upward and downward. Water, minerals, and fertilizer are absorbed from the roots through the process of transpiration, which takes place in the leaves. The leaves also make food, through photosynthesis, which is then transported downwards in the phloem. This same process removes carbon dioxide from the air and transforms it into oxygen, which is then released back into the environment.

Opposite page
Callistemon viminalis
Weeping bottlebrush tree flower

Trees

Left
Cassia javanica
Pink shower tree flowers

Introduction to trees

Surat Al-Naml, Verse 60:
[More precisely], is He [not best] who created the heavens and the earth and sent down for you rain from the sky, causing to grow thereby gardens of joyful beauty which you could not [otherwise] have grown the trees thereof? Is there a deity with Allah? [No], but they are a people who ascribe equals [to Him].

Members of the tree group are some of the largest, tallest, and most long-lived of plant species. Trees are woody perennial plants, and can be either deciduous or evergreen. They show great variety in shape and height depending on the species, ranging from dwarf cultivars that are only 1m in height to towering trees that grow to over 90m tall. On average, trees are classified as being usually over 6m in height, and tending to develop a distinct crown. They usually have a single woody stem, called a trunk, although some trees can have two or three stems. When a tree is cut, rings can be seen in the cross-section of the trunk. These rings tell us about the life of the tree; lighter rings describe seasons when the tree grew quicker, and darker rings show slower growth, perhaps during summer or autumn seasons. The older a tree, the more rings can be seen. Some trees live for thousands of years.

Importance of trees: From the beginning of time, trees have provided people with food, in the form of fruits and nuts, which can supply all the nutrients needed for life and growth. Planting trees also provides an important source of food and shelter for birds and other wildlife. This is mentioned in the Holy Quran:

Surat As-Sajdah, Verse 27:
Have they not seen that We drive the water [in clouds] to barren land and bring forth thereby crops from which their livestock eat and [they] themselves? Then do they not see?

Trees are a source of wood and paper. This is mentioned in the Holy Quran:

Surat Luqman, Verse 27:
And if whatever trees upon the earth were pens and the sea [was ink], replenished thereafter by seven [more] seas, the words of Allah would not be exhausted. Indeed, Allah is Exalted in Might and Wise.

Trees are a source of charcoal and other illuminants such as oil. This is mentioned in the Holy Quran:

Surat Ya-Seen, Chapter 36, Verse 80:
[It is] He who made for you from the green tree, fire, and then from it you ignite.

Opposite page
Boswellia sacra
Frankincense flowers

Trees provide people with industrial materials such as fiber, cork, gum, wax, and oil, as well as medicines, including aspirin, quinine, and cocaine.

Trees are important to our quality of life, whether they are planted in private gardens or in public areas. They are planted for many different reasons—for their appearance (shape, kind of leaves, color, smell), for food production, and most importantly in the Middle East, to provide shade.

Most bees build hives in trees. Bees eat pollen from the flowers of the tree they inhabit, as well as neighboring trees, giving people honey, with all its health and curative properties. This is mentioned in the Holy Quran:

Surat An-Nahl, Chapter 16, Verse 68:
And your Lord inspired to the bee, "Take for yourself among the mountains, houses, and among the trees and [in] that which they construct."

Trees can be used to create boundaries in the garden, and also to hide unattractive features such as to block out the view of a busy road.

Planting trees in public areas such as parks, or in private spaces such as home gardens, is like installing a natural air conditioning and heating system. In the summer the leaves of deciduous trees absorb sunlight and give shade, reducing the ambient temperature of the area. In cooler weather, when the tree branches are bare, sunlight is let through, warming the area.

Trees, when properly placed, can be used to control wind-flow patterns, and can absorb and reduce the force of wind on surrounding areas. For example, conifers such as cypress trees, when planted in rows along a given space, are natural windbreaks, and also act as a living privacy fence.

Trees can increase road safety. Many traffic accidents are caused by driver's exceeding the speed limit. Speeding is more of a problem on empty roads, where drivers increase their speed unknowingly because their eyes have no point of reference. When trees are planted along roadsides and in meridians, they provide the illusion that cars are travelling faster than their actual speed, thus causing drivers to slow down. In the Gulf region, palm trees are often planted for this purpose.

Trees, through their root systems, fix the soil they are planted in and prevent desert sands from encroaching on cities. They can also help to conserve water, and their roots prevent soil from being washed away by heavy rains.

No matter what the reason for planting trees, in doing so we have the power to positively change the local climate.

Planting trees: When planting trees around the home, there are some simple guidelines to follow. It is essential to leave a 3–4m gap between trees and any walls surrounding the property. Trees of similar type should be planted together, as they have the same water and fertilizer requirements. Trees should be planted 1–2m apart, depending on the type of tree, and saplings should be placed in holes at least 1m deep. Most tree saplings need to be supported in the first years to protect them from the wind.

To support young trees, install 1–2m long stakes in the ground approximately 10–15cm away from the tree trunk. This distance is required to ensure that the tree's root system is not damaged. Bind the stakes to the tree in at least three separate places, for equal lateral support.

Caring for trees:

Pruning: Pruning is an important procedure to protect the health of the tree; if neglected, the tree will grow in an unbalanced fashion. Pruning removes sick, dry, and dead branches, allowing the tree to direct its energy towards new, healthy growth. The best time to prune is in the autumn and at the beginning of summer.

Fertilizer: Fertilizer is the food plants need to thrive. All trees need essential elements such as nitrogen, phosphorus, potassium, magnesium, manganese, and boron to grow. The best, most well-rounded fertilizer for trees is NPK; this can be purchased from any plant nursery. To fertilize trees, inject fertilizer into the soil surrounding the tree, where the roots have spread. Make holes in the soil, 30–60cm deep, in a circle around the tree, with the radius of the circle a distance of 70–100cm from the trunk. Space each hole 30–60cm apart. Fertilize deciduous trees in spring when new growth can be seen, and evergreen trees twice a year, in autumn and spring.

Diseases and insects: Like any living thing, trees can be afflicted by illness or insects. These issues should be immediately addressed, with the help of a specialist if necessary.

Wounds: Trees can be wounded by people, animals, cars, and strong winds. Any injury to the trunk or branches of a tree should be treated immediately; if left unattended, infection can set in. To treat a wound, first clean the gash completely, removing all dead and damaged tissue. Next, cover the wound with a salve to protect it from bacterial and fungal infection. Finally, if the wound is very deep it must be filled with cement or a special plastic that the plant cannot absorb. This is done to prevent rot. Wounds of this type are best treated by experienced gardeners.

Tree reproduction: Like other types of plants, all trees have flowers, by which they reproduce. The egg of the tree is in the pistil of the flower, and it is fertilized by the pollen of the stamen. This produces the seed, which will grow into a new tree. Most trees have bisexual flowers, which means the same flower has both male and female structures. Some trees are monoecious, which means they produce separate male and female flowers, but both are on the same tree. Cypress (*Cupressus*) and fig (*Ficus*) are examples of monoecious trees. Less common are dioecious trees, plants which have only male flowers on one tree, and only female flowers on another. If trees are dioecious, male and female trees must be planted in proximity to one another to reproduce. Date palms (*Phoenix dactylifera*) are examples of dioecious plants. All trees require assistance with pollination; pollen is usually transferred by the wind, by insects (such as bees), or by birds or other animals.

Types of trees: Trees serve as a framework for gardens, a structure around which a personal oasis can be built. They come in a wide variety of colors, sizes, and shapes. Understanding the different types of trees available will help in planning a garden landscape.

Conifers: Coniferous trees often have a vaguely triangular shape; in these species the trunk of the tree grows faster than the side branches grow out, and the leaves produce a fuller shape on the lower branches. Also, the branches of the tree are generally shorter as they grow up the trunk. Coniferous trees do not require pruning, and are attractive when planted along the sides of a house. An example of a coniferous tree is the Italian cypress.

Flowering trees: Flowering trees are colorful additions to any garden. These trees are attractive as specimens, and are best placed under balconies or near terraces. Examples of flowering trees are the frangipani tree (*Plumeria spp.*) and the orchid tree (*Bauhinia spp.*).

Fragrant trees: Fragrant trees add another sensory dimension to gardens, as their delicate scent can often be smelled from a distance. Examples of fragrant trees are neem (*Azadirachta indica*), albizia (*Albizia lebbeck*), and tree jasmine (*Millingtonia hortensis*).

Fruit-bearing trees: In addition to their attractive foliage and fragrant blossoms, fruit-bearing trees provide an edible, healthy harvest. Examples of fruit-bearing trees include Assyrian plum (*Cordia myxa*) and fig (*Ficus spp.*).

Open-headed trees: The branches of open-headed trees grow in such a way as to give the tree an umbrella-like shape. An example of this is the royal poinciana (*Delonix regia*).

Round-headed trees: Round-headed trees get their name from the dome shape of their crowns. These stately trees have broad leaves, and can be planted as specimens in large gardens. An example of a round-headed tree is the neem tree (*Azadirachta indica*).

Weeping trees: Weeping trees are named for their drooping branches. This type of tree, when fully grown, usually has a large circumference, and takes up ample land space. Therefore, it is better to plant weeping trees individually, rather than in pairs or clusters. These dramatic plants are beautiful when placed near water, such as swimming pools or ponds. Examples of weeping trees are bottle brush (*Callistemon spp.*) and weeping myall (*Acacia pendula*).

Columnar trees: The leaves on this type of tree grow at an even rate on both the bottom and the top, giving the tree its columnar shape. This type of tree has tissue at the top that allows the plant to experience faster upward growth than lateral growth. Columnar trees do not require pruning; they naturally grow in a balanced, symmetrical shape. These trees are best planted in rows as a natural windbreak, or as a fence to delineate different sections of the garden. An example of a columnar tree is the horsetail tree (*Casuarina spp.*).

Opposite page
Delonix regia
Flame tree flowers

Acacia
Wattle

Acacia is a large genus of over 1,100 species of deciduous and evergreen trees, large shrubs, and climbers. The majority of the trees in this genus are native to Australia, and almost all grow in desert areas. *Acacias* range in size from large shrubs to tall trees, reaching 2–30m in height and 2–7m in girth. These attractive plants may be grown for their flowers or their greenery. They have finely divided foliage with small, attractive, bi-pinnate leaves. Most *Acacias* feature yellow or white pom-pom-like flowers that bloom in spring. Their heady, sweet scent is strong and can often be smelled from a distance. In some species new foliage will appear after the flowers have faded. *Acacias* are adaptable trees, suitable for gardens with average soils. However, these trees require careful pruning after first planting, to establish an attractive shape.

Acacia trees are considered one of the most successful types of tree grown in the Arabian Gulf, as many are native to the region and have adapted to the extreme environmental conditions present there. These perennial trees are planted in settled desert areas as a natural barrier to prevent sand from encroaching on cities. They are also used to hold and enrich coastal soil.

The following are the most common *Acaia* species grown in the Arabian Gulf region:

***Acacia dealbata*, silver wattle, mimosa:** Native to Australia, the silver wattle is a majestic evergreen tree growing 15–30m tall and 6–10m wide. The silver wattle has full, attractive foliage consisting of fern-like, bi-pinnate, hairy leaves, each about 12cm long, composed of 40–80 linear, glaucous to silvery leaflets. This tree produces 10–20cm long terminal racemes of spherical, fragrant pale lemon-yellow flowerheads. Each dainty bloom is 5mm across, growing in axillary racemes 4–8cm long, which are clustered towards the tips of the stems.

Opposite page
Acacia pendula
Weeping myall flowers

Above
Acacia nilotica
Arabian acacia flowers

Above
Acacia nilotica
Arabian acacia

Acacia farnesiana **(synonym *Vachellia farnesiana*), sweet acacia, needle bush:** Native to Central America, including Mexico, sweet acacia is a small, multi-trunk tree or shrub. It is widespread in other parts of the world including Asia and Australia. Reaching a mature height of 4.5–9m, and spreading to an overall width of 6–7m, this deciduous tree is considered part of the legume family. *Acacia farnesiana* has been planted throughout the world, and is often considered a weed. Several species of birds use the plant for nesting and cover, and insects eat the nectar from its flowers.

Acacia farnesiana takes its other common name, needle bush, from the numerous thorns distributed along its branches. This plant has bi-pinnate leaves, 5–8cm in length. Each leaf has 10–12 pinnae, and each pinnae is composed of 15–40 linear-oblong leaflets. This foliage serves as a backdrop for the trees fragrant, solitary, spherical, pale yellow flowers, which appear in February and March. *Acacia farnesiana* blossoms are hermaphroditic, containing both male and female reproductive organs. The flowers are followed by smooth, brown, nearly cylindrical seedpods, 5–7cm long, each containing two seeds embedded in dry, spongy tissue. Sweet acacia are hardy plants, with a natural lifespan of 25–50 years.

Acacia nilotica **(synonym *Aracia arabica*), Arabian acacia, thorn mimosa, gum arabic, anber:** Arabian acacia, also often known as mimosa, is native to much of tropical and subtropical Africa, the Arabian Peninsula, and the regions of India and Pakistan. It is widely naturalized in many drier parts of the world and is considered invasive in Australia. In the Arabian Peninsula these drought-tolerant plants grow in the harsh Nejd and Rub Al Khali areas. This species has adapted to the desert environment by developing the ability to send down roots over 80m to search for water.

Arabian acacias are wonderful for outdoor gardens. They usually present as large shrubs or small trees, measuring 5–15m in height. When used in landscaping these plants require frequent, bi-monthly pruning to achieve a pleasing, symmetrical shape. The foliage of the mimosa consists of bi-pinnate leaves, about 12cm long, each with 16–20 fine, 1cm long leaflets. These leaflets are carried on each leaf, which branches out from the side branches.

Above
Acacia nilotica
Arabian acacia leaves

These branches also produce 2–3cm long thorns. In the desert this foliage provides nourishment for camels, which have the unique ability to place their mouths over the stem and strip off the leaves without being punctured by the thorns. The bark of these trees is dark in color, and produces a kind of gum. Acacia trees have small, axillary flowers. These yellow, fluffy, ball-like spring blossoms are not as showy as other acacias, yet they are so fragrant they can be smelled from a distance. They are a favorite of bees, who are attracted to these flowers to gather nectar for honey. Once the flowers have faded, seed pods appear.

With careful pruning, *Acacia nilotica* can also be grown as an indoor plant. To be grown as a full shrub, the outer branches should be pruned. To encourage taller plant growth, cut the lower branches, and add support to the trunk of the shrub.

***Acacia pendula*, weeping myall:** Native to Australia, the weeping myall is a bushy, broad-headed, evergreen tree, reaching a full height of between 6 and 10m, and an overall width of 6–7m. This fast-growing tree has pendent branches filled with lance- or slightly sickle-shaped, greyish green to glaucous leaves, which are actually pendulous, flattened stems known as phyllodes. Each phyllode grows to a length of about 10cm. From winter through to spring the weeping myall produces small clusters of round, creamy yellow flowers. Each small blossom is only 1cm in diameter, and is borne from the phyllode axils in short, branching racemes, 2–5cm long. These colorful flowers attract birds.

***Acacia tortilis* (synonym *Vachellia tortilis*), umbrella thorn acacia, Samar tree:** A small, wiry, multi-stemmed shrub or tree, the umbrella thorn acacia reaches a full height of 5–21m and spreads 8–13m wide. Known in its native East Africa and the Middle East as the Samar tree, this plant may have a rounded or flat-topped crown, and is one of the most widespread trees in this seasonally dry area. The tree's crown and its very long thorns

Above
Acacia farnesiana
Sweet acacia resin, fruit and leaves

give the tree its popular common name. The umbrella thorn acacia features two types of thorns, one long and straight and the other short and hooked, growing singly or in pairs. Ranging from 1.2–8cm in length, it is these thorn characteristics that distinguish this tree from other *Acacia* species in Africa and the Middle East.

Acacia tortilis has a trunk covered in rough bark that is grey to dark brown or black in color. This trunk supports branches featuring foliage consisting of bi-pinnate leaves, with two to 10 pairs of pinnae, each with up to 15 pairs of leaflets. The foliage of the Samar tree is smaller than in many acacias, with leaves only 2.5cm long. When in bloom this tree produces small white or cream-colored flowers. These highly aromatic blossoms, with heads only 1cm in diameter, grow in tight clusters. Spent flowers are followed by pods containing up to 14 greenish brown seeds. These pods may be flat, spirally-twisted, or, rarely, almost straight; the pods are 8–12cm long and 6–10mm wide, and are gold brown in color.

Care: *Acacia* trees are a viable choice for Gulf gardens, as they thrive in full sun or partial shade and are tolerant of salty soil, high temperatures, and heavy humidity. They do, however, require frequent fertilization with a water soluble fertilizer, as well as regular watering. *Acacia* trees should be pruned at least once a year to encourage a denser crown and a more pleasing shape.

Propagation: From seed. Soak seeds in warm water until swollen and plant directly into the ground, 1cm deep.

Pests and diseases: Members of the *Acacia* genus are susceptible to red spider mite damage. These pests should be treated by a licensed exterminator.

Uses: Several parts of the *Acacia* tree are useful, and serve many medicinal and industrial purposes. The bark of this tree can be ground into a powder which, when mixed with water into a paste, can be applied as

Above
Acacia pendula
Weeping myall tree and leaves

an antiseptic for cuts and foot wounds. This mixture, when warmed, can also be applied as a poultice to soothe muscle pain. One tablespoon of ground *Acacia* bark mixed with one cup of water and boiled for 10 minutes makes a soothing, cleansing gargle. This gargle can be used up to four times a day to treat inflammation of the gums and throat. The gummy roots of this tree have also been chewed as a treatment for sore throat.

Acacia trees are a popular source of wood. This wood is heavy, hard, durable and close-grained. It is used for fencing posts, agricultural implements, pegs, and woodenware. The woody branches of the *Acacia farnesiana* species are used in India as tooth brushes, and the trees have also been used for erosion control in sandy soils. The bark and the fruit of *Acacia farnesiana* are a source of tannin, which is used in making dyes and inks.

Acacia trees produce a substance called gum. This gum, made from the sap or resin of the *Acacia* tree, is mixed with limestone and salt to make gum arabic. Historically, *Acacia nilotica* was probably the original source of the substance, although it is now commercially obtained from *Acacia senegal* or *Acacia seyal*; both of these species are also considered ornamental in their own right. Gum arabic is an incredibly versatile substance. Medicinally, it can be used to treat many conditions, including coughing and other respiratory ailments. A decoction of the gum from the trunk of the *Acacia farnesiana* species has been used in the treatment of diarrhea. Gum arabic has been used in cancer treatments, to stimulate kidney and liver function, and as a treatment for high blood pressure and diabetes. It is also a natural alternative to antibiotics, and has even been used to set broken bones. Gum arabic, when mixed with Arabic oil, can be used in the treatment of hemorrhoids. If mixed with rosewater, it can be placed in the eyes to treat conjunctivitis. In food production, Gum arabic is used as a binding agent, in items

Opposite page

Acacia ehrenbergiana
Salam tree and flowers

Above

Acacia tortilis
Samar flowers and tree

such as chewing gum and candy. This sticky substance is also used in cigarette paper, and on the closure of envelopes. Gum arabic is used in many other products and processes, including cosmetics, water paints, paint for shoes, and photographic printing.

The leaves of *Acacia farnesiana* are used in cooking as a tamarind flavoring for chutneys, and the pods are roasted for use in sweet and sour dishes. Medicinally, the tree's leaves can be rubbed on the skin to treat skin diseases. The powdered dried leaves can be applied externally as a treatment for wounds. The flowers of this species of *Acacia* are also useful, both in medicine and in cosmetics. An essential oil, called Cassie, is distilled from these blossoms, and is widely used in the perfume industry in Europe. Topically, the flowers are added to an ointment which is rubbed on the forehead to treat headaches. Internally, an infusion of the blossoms can be taken to treat dyspepsia and other stomach ailments. *Acacia* blossoms are also attractive to foraging bees.

The ripe seeds of *Acacia farnesiana* are put through a press to make oil for cooking. A gummy substance obtained from the young pods is used to mend broken pottery. *Acacia* seeds also have medicinal properties and are used to treat a wide variety of conditions. Ground to a powder and mixed with water, they can be applied to reduce the inflammation of hemorrhoids. Taken internally they have anthelmintic properties, and are used to cleanse the digestive tract and rid the body of intestinal parasites.

Finally, some species of *Acacia* are a vital source of food for foraging animals in semi-arid regions. *Acacia farnesiana* is a significant source of forage in many areas, with a protein content around 18%. *Acacia tortilis* provides food for both wild and domesticated animals, and is a staple in the diet of camels and goats. Its pods and leaves provide substantial levels of digestible protein and energy, as well as being rich in minerals. The seeds of this tree are high in crude protein and phosphorus.

Opposite page
top row
Acacia sclerosperma
Silver bark wattle tree and flowers

Opposite page
bottom row
Acacia farnesiana
Sweet acacia tree, leaves and thorns

Above
Acacia iteaphylla
Willow wattle

32

Left to right
Acacia nilotica
Arabian acacia fruit;
Acacia iteaphylla
Willow wattle fruit;
Acacia sclerosperma
Silver bark wattle fruit;
Acacia farnesiana
Sweet acacia fruit

Left
Acacia tortilis
Samar tree

Adansonia digitata
African Baobab Tree, Upside-down Tree

Adansonia is a small genus of about 10 species of deciduous trees. Members of this genus are native to tropical and semi-arid regions of Africa and Australia.

***Adansonia digitata*, African baobab tree:** Native to Africa south of the Sahara, *Adansonia digitata* is the most widespread of the *Adansonia* species on the African continent, and is commonly known as the African baobab tree. This species is able to survive in harsh, arid climates due to a shallow, wide-spreading root system. Growing out from the base of the plant further in diameter than the height of the tree, these roots collect and store massive amounts of water.

A slow-growing perennial, the African baobab tree has a lifespan of several hundred years. It has a bottle-shaped trunk which can reach a diameter of 2–14m. The thick, succulent trunk is smooth, shiny, and is covered in a cork-like bark that ranges from reddish brown to grey in color. Reaching a full height of 5–30m and supporting a rounded crown with a mature spread of 30m, *Adansonia digitata* is considered the largest succulent plant in the world.

The African baobab tree has foliage which consists of rounded, palmately compound leaves. These leaves, clustered at the ends of short, thick, wide branches, usually grow in sets of five to nine oblong-elliptic leaflets, dark green in color, 12–17cm long. Since the African baobab is a deciduous tree, it sheds its leaves during the winter months and produces new growth in the late spring or early summer. In the winter, when the tree is bare, its spreading branches resemble roots. This seasonal appearance gives the tree its other common name, the upside-down tree.

Opposite page
Adansonia digitata
African baobab
tree flower

Above
Adansonia digitata
African baobab tree

Right
Adansonia digitata
African baobab tree

From October to December, the African baobab produces dramatic, solitary, pendent flowers. These blossoms emerge in the late afternoon from large round buds on drooping stalks. The flowers are 10–12cm across, with partially reflexed, five-crinkled, waxy, creamy white petals. These petals surround stamens that emerge as an extended cluster of balls. Sweetly scented when in bloom, the flowers fall within 24 hours, turning brown and developing a foul odor. *Adansonia digitata* blossoms are pollinated by bats, insects, and the wind. The tree is usually between eight and 23 years old before its first flowering.

Aside from African baobab and upside-down tree, *Adansonia digitata* takes several of its other colloquial names from its fruit. It is known as the dead-rat tree, from the appearance of the fruit, the monkey-bread tree, from the fruits' soft, dry texture, and the cream of tartar tree, from the fruit's acidic taste. In the Sudan, the fruit is known as gangalese. Each large, cylindrical capsule is 10–35cm long and 13cm wide, and covered with yellowish brown hairs. The fruit has a durable, woody outer shell and a dry, powdery pulp inside. It contains 100 hard, black, kidney-shaped seeds.

Care: African baobab is occasionally planted as a street tree and in city parks, although it is also a good choice for large desert gardens. These trees thrive in full sun or partial shade and are tolerant of the salty, sandy Gulf soil.

African baobab trees are resistant to drought, although during the growing season they do require a monthly application of a low-phosphate liquid fertilizer.

Propagation: *Adansonia digitata* are seldom available in nurseries, and are most commonly propagated from cuttings or by seed. Seeds can be collected from dry fruits by cracking the fruit open and washing away the dry, powdery coating. Soak seeds in a container of hot water for 24 hours, then allow to cool. Seeds are best sown in spring and summer, in a well-drained seedling mixture containing one-third sand. Bury seeds 4–6mm deep, and place trays in a warm, semi-shaded location. Water regularly until all seeds have germinated; this may take

Above
Adansonia digitata
African baobab tree
flower and fruits

anywhere from two or three weeks to six months. During this time, seedlings should be carefully monitored for damping off fungus, which can be treated with a fungicidal drench.

Pests and diseases: African baobab trees are susceptible to aphid damage. These pests may infest young leaves and flower buds. They should be treated by a licensed exterminator.

Uses: *Adansonia digitata* holds great social and economic importance in its indigenous regions. All parts of the tree are used by local people, offering protection and providing food, clothing and medicine, as well as raw material for many useful items. The worldwide demand for resources from the baobab tree has increased dramatically in many sectors, including the food, medical, and cosmetic industries.

The African baobab is a traditional food plant in Africa. The tree is a source of fine quality honey; wild bees perforate the soft wood and lodge their honey in the holes. The leaves, flowers, fruit pulp, seeds, roots, and bark of the baobab are edible, and they have been studied by scientists for their useful properties. The leaves are said to be rich in vitamin C, sugars, potassium tartrate, and calcium. They are cooked fresh as a vegetable, or can be dried and crushed for later use. The sprout of a young tree can be eaten like asparagus, and the roots of very young trees are also edible. The seeds of *Adansonia digitata* are edible and can be roasted for use as a coffee substitute. They are a good source of phosphorus, calcium, zinc, sodium, iron, manganese, potassium, and magnesium.

Perhaps the most important food product of the baobab is its fruit. The fruit pulp is dry, can dissolve in water and milk, and may be incorporated into cold and hot drinks. This liquid is used as a lemonade-like drink, a sauce for food, and as a fermentation agent in local brewing. The fruit pulp is rich in vitamin C, calcium, phosphorus, carbohydrates and soluble and insoluble fibers.

Adansonia digitata is also an important food source for local animals, both wild and domestic. Caterpillars, which feed on the leaves, are collected and eaten by African people as an important source of protein. Wild animals eat the fallen leaves, and fresh leaves serve as quality fodder for domestic animals. Fallen flowers are eaten by wild animals and cattle alike.

The African baobab tree has a long history of medicinal use. Various parts of the plant are used for multiple medicinal purposes throughout Africa, as well as in other areas. Both the leaves and seeds are high in vitamin C and calcium, which strengthen the immune system. The leaves are used to treat kidney and bladder disease, asthma, and insect bites. The bark and seeds can be used to treat fevers and malaria. The seeds produce an oil which has pharmaceutical, nutritional, and industrial uses.

In addition to food and medicine, the many parts of *Adansonia digitata* serve practical purposes for people residing in its indigenous regions. The wood of the baobab is soft, light yellow and spongy, and is used for making boxes. The inner layer underneath the bark of the trunk yields a strong fiber, which can be used for making ropes and nets, and woven into cloth. The fruit pulp is burned to repel insects that plague domestic cattle. The trunks have been made into canoes, and glue can be manufactured from their flower's pollen. Large baobab trees with hollow stems have been used by people for centuries for various purposes, providing both water and shelter. The roots of the baobab can be tapped for water, and these trees have been the location of prisons, pubs, storage barns, and even bus stops.

Opposite page
Adansonia digitata
African baobab tree

Albizia
Silk Tree

Native to tropical America, Indomalaya, Southeast Asia and northern Australia, *Albizia* is a genus of about 140 species of deciduous trees, shrubs, and climbers.

The following are the most common *Albizia* species grown in the Arabian Gulf region:

***Albizia julibrissin* f. *rosea*, silk tree:** Native to southern Asia, from Iran through China to Japan, *Albizia julibrissin* is commonly grown as a large shrub or small tree. Reaching a maximum height of 6m and spreading to a width of 4–6m, this tree develops a full, domed crown when mature. Its foliage consists of fern-like, light to mid-green leaves, 30–45cm long, composed of many small, sickle-shaped leaflets. Colloquially known as silk tree, in the summer this plant produces terminal clusters, each 7–15cm wide, of spherical, pink flowerheads. Each blossom is about 3.5cm in diameter.

***Albizia lebbeck*, mother's tongue tree:** This deciduous species ranges from 10–25m in height, and is grown for both its filigree foliage and attractive flowerheads of small florets with long stamens, which appear on

Opposite page
Albizia lebbeck
Mother's tongue tree flowers

Above
Albizia lebbeck
Mother's tongue tree

Above
Albizia lebbeck
Mother's tongue tree

trees only a few years after planting. The mother's tongue tree has dramatic, dark green leaves, bi-pinnate with many oblong-ovate to sickle-shaped leaflets. These leaves close if they are touched by hand or by raindrops, and also close together at night.

Albizia lebbeck produces fragrant blossoms in white, yellow, or greenish-yellow. These flowers give way to long, narrow, pod-shaped fruits, about 30cm long, each holding four to 12 brown seeds, which are used for propagation.

Care: *Albizia* trees are able to thrive in the Gulf region, as they can grow in full sun or partial shade and are tolerant of salty soil. However, these plants require regular watering, as well as monthly fertilization with a water soluble fertilizer.

Propagation: From seed. Soak seeds in warm water until swollen before planting. This tree can also be propagated by rooting semi-ripe cuttings with bottom heat in summer.

Pests and diseases: *Albizia lebbeck* is susceptible to red spider mite and whitefly. These pests should be treated by a licensed exterminator.

Uses: The pod-shaped fruits of the mother's tongue tree can be used as cattle fodder, and its wood can be used in factories. Historically, this plant was also used in traditional medicine in southern Asia.

Above top row
Albizia julibrissin f. *rosea*
Silk tree leaves and flower

Above bottom row
Albizia lebbeck
Mother's tongue tree leaves and fruits

Azadirachta indica
Neem Tree

Azadirachta is a genus composed of only two distinct species of trees. These plants are native to southern Asia, spreading as far as East India, and can even be found in Sri Lanka. It is widely cultivated outside its natural range, often as a street tree.

***Azadirachta indica*, neem tree:** The neem tree is an open-branched, round-headed evergreen. Once it reaches maturity, about eight years after planting, this large tree can attain heights of 15–20m, and its light grey trunk may reach a diameter of up to 28cm. Neem foliage consists of alternate, bi-pinnate leaves. These leaves are composed of green, pointed leaflets with toothed edges, each 5–10cm long, which are divided into eight to 12 pairs. The total leaf size is 20–40cm, and a midrib divides each leaf into two asymmetrical parts. Once a neem tree is three to four years old it produces fragrant blossoms in the summertime. These flowers are white, each consisting of five petals, and grow in clusters. Neem trees bloom from the end of March until May, when the flowers give way to berry-like fruits. Fruits mature at the end of June and the beginning of July. These fruits are ovate, green ripening to yellow in color, and contain seeds. Neem seeds have oil that is used for medicinal purposes. This oil is lost once the seeds dry out, approximately 21–30 days after appearing.

Neem trees are easily adaptable, and good for all kinds of climate and soil. They can tolerate a wide variety of weather conditions. These trees are commonly planted along streets and in parks because they have an attractive shape and are good for shade. This tree can also be planted on hillsides to hold the soil and protect against soil erosion. When planting multiple neem trees in a large garden or farm, place in rows, allowing at least 8m between each plant.

Opposite page
Azadirachta indica
Neem tree flowers

Above
Azadirachta indica
Neem tree

Right
Azadirachta indica
Neem tree

Care: Neem trees are hardy, salt-tolerant plants that can grow in any type of soil, be it sandy or muddy. This makes them an excellent choice for landscaping in the Gulf region.

However, although neem trees have the ability to thrive in a variety of conditions, they do require some special attention, particularly in the early years. Neem saplings require regular irrigation, consistent pruning, and supports to brace the trunk. Two pieces of wood can be used as stakes to support the tree, and these braces can be removed as the tree becomes established. Neem trees require both natural and chemical fertilizer once a year. Mix 10–15kg of natural fertilizer into the soil around the base of the tree, then water thoroughly. For chemical fertilization, add a fertilizer tablet to the soil.

Propagation: From seed. Soak seeds in water for 24 hours before planting. Neem seeds gradually lose their viability after the fruit is mature, so seeds should be harvested as soon as the fruit is ripe. If seeds are collected more than 45 days after the fruit has ripened, they are not usable for propagation. Neem trees can also be propagated by cutting or layering.

Pests and diseases: *Azadirachta indica* trees are susceptible to scale insect and mealy bug damage. These pests should be treated by a licensed exterminator.

Uses: The neem tree is incredibly valuable, and is regarded as one of the 500 most useful medicinal trees. Every part of the neem tree can be used in some product or process. The leaves are used for a variety of medicinal purposes. Boil the leaves to make a gargle for teeth and gums. This water can also be used as a rinse to stop hair loss, and encourages shiny, strong hair growth. Neem leaves are a natural insecticide. Leaves may be placed inside carpets or clothing when storing them to protect them from insects. These same dried leaves can also be placed in kitchen cabinets, in the pots of houseplants, or anywhere around the house to get rid of pests. Neem leaves are high in protein, and in India are used as cattle fodder. Neem seeds produce an oil that was once used as a light source. After extracting the oil from the seeds, the by-product left from the extraction process can be mixed with the tree's leaves to produce a natural fertilizer. The wood of the neem tree is used in making furniture, as it is resistant to termites. The bark of tree has a substance that can be used to color cotton and silk. This substance is also used in makeup, toothpaste, soap, and insecticides.

Above
Azadirachta indica
Neem tree leaves and fruits

Bambusa
Bamboo

Bamboo is found in tropical and subtropical Africa, Asia and is naturalized in parts of Central America. This plant belongs to the genus *Bambusa*, which consists of about 120 species of clump-forming, evergreen perennials, ranging in height from 3–25m and growing 4–10cm in diameter. Bamboo spreads quickly because it has rhizomatous roots that travel under the soil. This plant can be invasive, and can quickly take over the garden if not controlled.

The following are the most common *Bambusa* species grown in the Arabian Gulf region:

Bambusa tuldoides (synonym *Bambusa ventricosa*), Buddha's-belly bamboo: This species of bamboo, sometimes used in bonsai, gets its colloquial name from the internodal swelling that produces a series of bulges along the bamboo's stem. Pruning the tops of the culms of this plant, to restrict its upward growth, make these swellings more prominent. Buddha's-belly bamboo is a bushy, upright evergreen, with strong canes that can range in height from 5–25m and have an average diameter of 6cm. This plant's varying height range makes it useful for a wide variety of purposes, such as windbreaks, privacy screens, or, for smaller varieties, in containers. In addition to its unique cane structure, Buddha's belly features foliage consisting of whorls of 10–20 linear-lance-shaped, dark green leaves, each about 12cm long.

***Bambusa vulgaris*, golden bamboo:** Golden bamboo is a tall, vibrantly colored plant. It has lemon yellow, smooth, usually hollow canes, or stems, which are thick-walled, inflexible, and not easy to split. These stems can range in height from 10–20m,

Opposite page
Bambusa tuldoides
Buddha's-belly bamboo

Above
Bambusa tuldoides
Buddha's-belly bamboo
stem, leaves and roots

and are 4–10cm thick. They do not grow straight, but rather produce a series of nodes. At each node branches form, bearing linear-lance-shaped, green striped and dark green leaves.

Golden bamboo is often cultivated for its rich foliage, and grows well in full sunlight or partial shade. It thrives in humid climates, but can tolerate unfavorable conditions like low temperatures and drought. Golden bamboo grows mostly on river banks, road sides, and open ground, and can be used in the garden as a natural fence or border hedge. Young golden bamboo plants can be grown indoors as houseplants, in large containers.

Care: Bamboo trees thrive in full sun or partial shade and are tolerant of soil with a high salinity content, making them a feasible addition to gardens in the Gulf region. Once established they require little care; water moderately and fertilize sparingly.

Propagation: By dividing established clumps in springtime.

Pests and diseases: Bamboo plants are susceptible to slugs, and are prone to fungal diseases such as leaf rust and leaf spot. These conditions should be treated by an experienced gardener or a licensed exterminator.

Uses: All parts of the bamboo plant are useful. The stems can be burned as fuel, used in construction, and are even made into items such as kitchen utensils and canoes. Fibers from the trunks of these plants can be processed into paper. The hollow canes are used to make furniture, as well as smoking pipes and even irrigation pipes. The leaves are used as animal fodder, and are in fact the main source of food for the pandas of China. Young bamboo shoots can be cooked, pickled, or made into a soup, and are eaten throughout Asia. In many traditions across Asia they are said to have medicinal value.

Opposite page
Bambusa vulgaris
Golden bamboo

Above
Bambusa vulgaris
Golden bamboo stem and leaves

Bauhinia
Orchid Tree

A native of Latin America, tropical Africa, and southern Asia through to Australasia, the genus *Bauhinia* contains approximately 250 species of large and small trees, shrubs, and vines. The diversity of the plants in this group make it a favorite of gardeners.

Bauhinia trees include both evergreen and deciduous varieties, and they usually have twin-lobed leaves. These trees grow quickly from seed, and can range from 8 to 20m in height. *Bauhinia* trees shed their leaves as the plant's large, five-petalled, orchid-like flowers appear in spring, in shades of pure white, lavender, or pink.

The following are the most common *Bauhinia* species grown in the Arabian Gulf region:

Bauhinia x blakeana, Hong Kong orchid tree: Native to Hong Kong, and the national floral emblem of Hong Kong, *Bauhinia x blakeana* is a hybrid between *Bauhinia purpurea* and *Bauhinia variegata*. This quick-growing tree has a short multiple-stemmed trunk, dense canopy, and brittle medium-brown branches. At its mature height it is about 15m tall. *Bauhinia x blakeana* is sterile, and produces no seedpods. This unique tree has beautiful foliage, with alternate, palmate, simple, large, thick, double-lobed, green leaves, similar in shape to a heart or a butterfly. Leaves are normally 7–10cm long and about 10–13cm wide, with a deep cleft dividing the apex. Although this is naturally a multi-stemmed tree, it can be trained to grow with only a single trunk.

In addition to its striking foliage, the Hong Kong orchid tree produces dramatic orchid-like flowers in shades of purplish red or magenta, with a touch of white. Each blossom has a five-petalled corolla and tubular calyx, and measures 10–15cm in diameter. These blooms produce a noticeable fragrance during warm, humid days, and their scent attracts butterflies and bees to the garden. The Hong Kong orchid tree has the longest flowering season of all the trees in the *Bauhinia* genus,

Opposite page
Bauhinia x blakeana
Hong Kong orchid tree flowers

Above
Bauhinia x blakeana
Hong Kong orchid tree

Right
Bauhinia x blakeana
Hong Kong orchid tree

blooming from early November until late April, and sometimes through May.

***Bauhinia purpurea*, orchid tree:** Native to Southern China, the orchid tree is a small to medium-sized deciduous plant, reaching an adult height of only 15m. This petite tree has long, broad, rounded, alternate leaves, ranging from 10–20m in length, that are bi-lobed at the base and apex. *Bauhinia purpurea* produces fragrant, pink, five-petalled blossoms, which give way to fruit pods. Each pod measures about 30cm in length, and contains between 12 and 16 pea-sized seeds.

***Bauhinia variegata*, purple orchid tree:** Native to India and China, the purple orchid tree is a deciduous, spreading plant. This multi-trunk tree reaches a full height of 8–12m, and a width of 3–8m. The purple orchid tree has rich, dramatic foliage composed of vibrant green leaves, 10–20cm long, with heart-shaped bases and deeply two-lobed tips. It commonly bears short, terminal racemes of striking magenta, pink or purple flowers, each measuring 8–12cm in diameter. However, one variety of this stunning tree, *B. variegata* Candida, produces pure white blossoms. The purple orchid tree blooms from winter to summer.

Care: *Bauhinia* trees thrive in full sunlight, and actually require an abundance of sun to bloom well. New leaves will form as the flower blossoms fade. These trees also need ample water in dry conditions and must receive a monthly application of balanced liquid fertilizer. *Bauhinia* trees have an untidy growth habit, and regular, gentle pruning is required to help the plants maintain a neat shape.

Propagation: From seed. This tree is self-seeding. *Bauhinia* can also be propagated using cuttings, by grafting, and by air-layering.

Pests and diseases: *Bauhinia* are susceptible to red spider mite, mealy bug, aphid and whitefly. These pests should be treated by a licensed exterminator.

Uses: Various species of the *Bauhinia* tree are used for different purposes. *Bauhinia purpurea* is used in traditional Chinese medicine. In Hong Kong the leaves of *Bauhinia x blakeana* are known as "clever leaves," and are regarded as symbols of wisdom. People dry these leaves and make them into bookmarks, believing they will bring good luck in their studies.

Bauhinia x blakeana is particularly successful as specimen plants or in a garden border. Additionally, *Bauhinia x blakeana* blossoms make beautiful cut flowers. When placed in a bowl or vase, these blooms stay fresh for several days.

Above
Bauhinia
Orchid tree
leaves and fruits

Above
Bauhinia sp.
Orchid tree flowers

Opposite page
Bauhinia variegata Candida
White orchid tree flowers

Boswellia sacra
Frankincense, Olibanum Tree

Native to tropical regions of Africa and Asia, *Boswellia* is a genus of 40 or more species of dioecious, evergreen or drought-deciduous plants. It is from these moderately-sized, flowering trees and shrubs that the resinous dried sap used to make frankincense is harvested. There are several species and varieties of frankincense trees, each producing a slightly different type of resin. The scent and quality of frankincense is also influenced by the soil and climate in which the tree is grown. All trees in the *Boswellia* genus produce gum.

Boswellia sacra, frankincense tree, olibanum tree: Native to the Arabian Peninsula, including the countries of Oman and Yemen, as well as northeastern Africa, including Somalia, *Boswellia sacra* is a small evergreen or semi-deciduous tree. This plant may be single or multi-trunked; the texture of the bark is paper-like, and easily removable. Frankincense trees range between 2 and 8m in height, and feature foliage composed of alternate, compound leaves containing a number of elliptic leaflets. New leaves are covered with a fine down.

Boswellia sacra produces axillary clusters of tiny flowers. Each blossom is composed of five yellowish-white petals, 10 stamen and a cup with five teeth. The blooms are followed by small capsule-shaped fruit, measuring only 1cm in length.

Boswellia sacra is the most famous source of the oleo-gum-resin frankincense. Trees start producing resin when they are about

Opposite page
Boswellia sacra
Frankincense
tree flowers

Above
Boswellia sacra
Frankincense tree

Above
Boswellia sacra
Frankincense tree

eight to 10 years old. The resin is extracted by making a small, shallow incision on the trunk or branches of the tree, or by removing a portion of the bark. The resin is drained as a milky substance that coagulates in contact with air, and is collected by hand. Frankincense is collected in April; after the tree is scratched, the resin is left on the plant for 14 days, and then it is harvested. The first gum released by the tree is the best in quality; the harvesting procedure may be repeated, but the quality diminishes with each collection. Frankincense is usually harvested over a three-month period, with each tree producing about 10kg of gum per season.

Care: Frankincense trees are drought resistant, will grow in salty soil, and thrive in full sunlight. This makes them a perfect choice for Arabian Gulf landscapes.

Propagation: From seed.

Pests and diseases: Trees in the *Boswellia* genus are susceptible to attacks by the longhorn beetle. These pests should be treated by a licensed exterminator.

Uses: The foliage, flowers, and seedlings of *Boswellia* trees are used as animal fodder in Oman. However, the most widely used product of this plant is its resin. Frankincense has a long history of medicinal, religious and social uses. Essential oils are obtained by steam distillation of the dry resin, and these oils are used in perfumery and aromatherapy. They are also an ingredient in some skincare products. Medicinally, in Arab communities the gum is chewed to treat gastrointestinal ailments. It should not be swallowed, however, as digestion of the gum substance olianum can lead to stomach problems.

Above
Boswellia sacra Frankincense at various stages from resin to collection

Bucida molineti
Spiny Black Olive

Bucida is a genus of six species of spreading, evergreen trees which are native to North America, the Bahamas, Mexico, and Cuba. These plants, ranging in height from 2–12m, and spreading to a width of 12m, can be used for a variety of landscaping purposes; larger species are suitable for yards and gardens, while smaller varieties can be grown in containers. There are even types that are popular as bonsai plants.

Bucida molineti, spiny black olive: The spiny black olive is an attractive, hardy specimen. As a sapling the tree has a pyramidal shape, which rounds out as the tree matures, eventually developing a dense, oval to rounded crown. Once the tree reaches its maximum height it will continue to grow horizontally, and the crown may flatten. The spiny black olive features a smooth, grey-brown trunk from which grow strong, wind-resistant branches. These branches support the tree's dark, bluish-green, leathery foliage. Each leaf is 5–10cm long, alternate, simple, entire, and obovate to oblanceolate in shape. The leaves sprout in clusters at the branch tips, and sometimes intermingle with the spines that grow along the branches.

Although *Bucida molineti* is best known for its beautiful foliage, it also produces inconspicuous, small, greenish-yellow flowers. These tiny blossoms emerge in spikes in late spring or early summer. As the flowers fade, they are replaced by clusters of tiny, fleshy, flattened brown or black pod-like fruit. Each spiny olive pod is 20–30cm long and 1.5–2.5cm wide, and it is these fruits that give the tree its common name. While these pods are great for attracting bees, butterflies and birds to the garden, they also excrete a staining tannic acid material. This substance can damage patios, sidewalks, or vehicles, and should be considered when choosing a location for planting. A cultivar with attractive, white-variegated leaves is sometimes available commercially. This is *B. molinetii* Variegata.

Care: Spiny black olive trees are a viable choice for Gulf gardens, as they thrive in full sun or partial shade and are tolerant of salty soil. They do, however, require frequent fertilization with a water soluble fertilizer. These trees also need regular watering, and foliage will drop if the soil is left dry for too long.

Propagation: From seed. *Bucida molineti* can also be propagated by simple layering, air layering, or soft wood cuttings. If using cuttings, each specimen should be no longer than 3cm.

Pests and diseases: Trees in the *Bucida* genus are generally resistant to pests and diseases.

Uses: With its broad canopy, the spiny black olive is often planted to provide shade for other plants. The bark of the tree can be processed to produce a tanning agent, and wood from the tree's strong trunk is used to make lumber for house and fence construction, scaffolding, railroad ties, and pilings.

Opposite page
Bucida molineti
Spiny black olive

Butea monosperma
Flame of the Forest, Parrot Tree

Butea is a small genus of only four species of deciduous, flowering plants. Native to tropical and sub-tropical areas of the Indian subcontinent and Southeast Asia, this genus includes trees, shrubs, and climbers.

***Butea monosperma*, flame of the forest, parrot tree:** Indigenous to India, Sri Lanka, and Burma, *Butea monosperma* is a medium-sized, deciduous, perennial, ornamental tree. This slow-growing tree reaches a mature height of 5–15m, and a maximum spread of 3–5m. It has a crooked, twisted trunk, about 43cm in diameter, covered with rough, greyish-brown, fibrous bark that exudes a reddish substance. The trunk becomes more twisted with age.

This strongly branched tree features foliage consisting of alternate, compound, pinnate leaves composed of diamond-shaped to rounded, leathery, silky-backed leaflets. Each leaf is 10–20cm long, and is borne on stalks measuring 8–16cm in length. This greenery serves as a backdrop for the plant's colorful, pea-like flowers that emerge in showy, terminal racemes that are 5–40cm long. *Butea monosperma* takes one of its common names, the flame of the forest, from these bright orange-red, or more rarely yellow, flowers. Each flower is 2.5–4cm long, and consists of five petals comprising one standard, two smaller wings and a very curved beak-shaped keel. It is this keel which gives the plant its other common name, the parrot tree. Blossoms are borne along bare branches from winter to spring, and the flowers attract many butterflies and birds, which assist with pollination.

After flowering, *Butea monosperma* produces fruit in the form of flat pods, covered with short brown hairs. This fruit is pale yellowish-brown or grey when ripe, and measures 15–20cm long and 4–5cm wide. Each pod contains a single seed near the apex. The seed is ellipsoid, flattened, and about 3cm long. It contains a yellow fixed oil called moodooga oil.

Care: *Butea monosperma* trees are a good choice for gardens in the Arabian Gulf region, and also make beautiful specimen plants. They thrive in humid climates, and will grow in full sun or partial shade. These plants are drought resistant and can survive in salty soil. However, the soil should be enriched monthly with a balanced liquid fertilizer during the growing season.

Propagation: From seed in spring, or by rooting semi-ripe cuttings in summer.

Pests and diseases: Parrot trees are susceptible to red spider mite. These pests should be treated by a licensed exterminator.

Uses: *Butea monosperma* is used for timber, resin, animal fodder, dyes, and a variety of other industrial purposes. The wood of this tree is dirty white in color, soft, and durable under water. It is used for building well-curbs and making water scoops. The wood produces a good quality charcoal, and its pulp is used for newsprint manufacturing. Fibers from the bark of the trunk are used to make cordage. The leaves of the parrot tree are very leathery and are used by street food vendors as serving plates. Gum from the tree contains tannins

Opposite page
Butea monosperma
Flame of the forest flowers

Above
Butea monosperma
Flame of the forest

that are used in the leather industry, and are also used in some food preparations. This tree's distinctively colored flowers are used to make fabric dye. Flame of the forest trees and their flowers positively impact air pollution, and their blossoms serve to naturally control insects in any area they are planted. Historically, seeds from this plant were added to feed by Arab horse traders in order to keep their stock in good condition.

Butea monosperma is a traditional Indian medicinal tree. Various parts of this plant are used to treat a wide range of ailments including diabetes, eye-related diseases like cataracts, anemia in children, kidney stones, urinary blockages, and bladder pain. The flowers of this tree are most commonly used in the treatment of liver disorders, as well as in the treatment of inflammation, swelling, and sprains. For this purpose, flowers should be steam-cooked, and applied directly to the affected area. An infusion of parrot tree flowers can be taken to relieve diarrhea and urine retention. To prepare, take one handful of flowers and boil in one liter of water. Filter the mixture, add rock salt, and sip liquid frequently. A powder made from ground dried or fresh flowers can be taken to cleanse the body of toxins. Grind the petals with a mortar and pestle to make the powder, and take 1–2gm daily. Dried flowers are also used for the treatment of sexual dysfunction, intestinal infections, ulcers, and diabetes.

In addition to the flowers, the leaves, bark, seeds, gum and roots of this tree also have medicinal uses. The flowers and leaves of *Butea monosperma* are natural diuretics, aphrodisiacs, astringents, and they increase blood flow to the pelvic region. The leaves have been used to treat coughs, diabetes, menstruation issues, intestinal worms, piles, central nervous system disorders, and sexual debility, as well as the sensation of burning pain. The bark and seeds have been used in traditional concoctions which temporarily inhibit fertility. The seeds of this tree have diuretic properties, stimulating the production of urine. They also have purgative, anthelmintic, and anti-parasitic properties. For these purposes, fresh seed juice can be taken with honey. Seed powder can be used to treat intestinal parasites, and when ground with lemon juice it becomes a powerful rubefacient. In this form it causes dilation of the capillaries and increases blood circulation. The roots of the parrot tree have been used in the treatment of filariasis, night blindness, helminthiasis, piles, ulcers, and tumors. Gum powder from *Butea monosperma* can be used to treat diarrhea and dysentery. To prepare this medicine, mix 1/4 teaspoon of cinnamon powder and 1/4 teaspoon of gum powder and take with warm water. While the parrot tree is known for its medicinal properties, only a physician knowledgeable about the uses of this plant should administer the above treatments.

Above
Butea monosperma
Flame of the forest seeds and trees

Above

Butea monosperma
Flame of the forest
tree and flowers

Callistemon viminalis
Weeping Bottlebrush Tree

Callistemon is a small but diverse genus, belonging to a family of about 25 species of evergreen trees and shrubs. Trees in this group can vary from 1.5m to as much as 10m in height, and grow 2–5m wide. These willow-like plants feature small, greyish-green leaves, with foliage and flowers alternating on branches. Native to Australia, *Callistemon* is known for its drooping spikes of vibrant blossoms, which vary in color from bright red, pink, or creamy white, to purple, green, or yellow. These trees take their common name from their flowers, which are borne on young twigs, making them look like large bottle-brushes. This tree also bears brown, bead-like seeds that grow out of woody, cone-shaped capsules.

Callistemon is a perfect choice for Middle Eastern gardens, as it thrives in dry regions, and actually flowers less in wet soil. Bottle brush trees can be planted in shrub borders, but are also attractive features when planted alone, in full sun. These trees can be shaped by pruning, to encourage a fuller, denser crown.

***Callistemon viminalis*, weeping bottlebrush:** *Callistemon viminalis* is commonly named for its arch-shaped, "weeping" stems. This small tree measures 2–10m in height and spreads 1.5–4m wide. It can be grown as a small tree or bushy shrub, and can be planted in clusters in the garden. These plants feature attractive mid- to dark green leaves. Each simple, alternate leaf grows from 2–6cm long, is lance-shaped, glandular, and has a leathery texture. The weeping bottlebrush flowers from spring to summer, producing spikes of bright red blossoms. Each spike ranges from 10–20cm in length.

Care: Bottlebrush trees flourish in dry locations and should be planted in a location receiving full sun throughout the day. These trees are hardy, and can be pruned regularly to encourage a denser crown and a pleasing shape.

Propagation: From seed. *Callistemon* trees can also be propagated using cuttings.

Pests and diseases: Bottlebrush trees are susceptible to damage by red spider mite, scale insect, and mealy bug, all of which should be treated by a licensed exterminator.

Opposite page
Callistemon viminalis
Weeping bottlebrush flowers

Opposite page
Callistemon viminalis
Weeping bottlebrush

Left
Callistemon viminalis
Weeping bottlebrush
flower, leaves and fruits

Cascabela thevetia
Yellow Oleander

Native to North and South America, *Cascabela* is a genus of about five species of evergreen shrubs and small trees that feature attractive foliage in the form of alternate, simple, mostly linear to ovate leaves. They are cultivated, however, for their showy, funnel-shaped flowers. These blossoms, consisting of five over-lapping petals, emerge singly or in cymes.

***Cascabela thevetia* (synonym *Thevetia peruviana*), yellow oleander:** Originating in the tropical regions of the Americas, the yellow oleander is one of the most widely grown evergreen perennials in the Middle East. This delicate, erect, open shrub or occasionally small tree, reaches a height of 2–8m and spreads to a width of 1–3m. It features lustrous, narrowly lance-shaped, mid- to dark green leaves, ranging in length from 8–15cm. This attractive foliage is a wonderful contrast for the plant's small, single, trumpet-shaped, slightly fragrant flowers. The blossoms, while commonly yellow, also come in apricot-colored or almost white varieties. After the flowers fade, small, apple-like fruits appear, turning black as they ripen.

Cascabela thevetia is a hardy plant and should be pruned quite vigorously, once a year in autumn or spring, to maintain it as a bushy shrub. If left to grow naturally, the yellow oleander will become a small shade tree. Gardeners enjoy some flexibility in the placement of *Cascabela thevetia*, as this tree thrives equally well in full sun or partial shade.

Caution: The leaves, flowers, fruit, and white latex substance exuded by this plant when cut are all extremely poisonous.

Care: *Cascabela* trees flourish in dry locations where they can receive full sun all day. They require little special care, aside from ample water and applications of a balanced liquid fertilizer monthly during the growing season. These trees are robust, and can be pruned regularly to maintain a pleasant shape and encourage a denser crown.

Propagation: From seed or cuttings.

Pests and diseases: Plants found in the *Cascabela* genus are susceptible to aphid damage. These pests should be treated by a licensed exterminator.

Opposite page
Cascabela thevetia
Yellow oleander flower

Above
Cascabela thevetia
Yellow oleander
leaves and fruit

Right
Cascabela thevetia
Yellow oleander
flowers and trees

Cassia
Cassia Tree

Cassia is a small genus of approximately 30 species of evergreen or deciduous shrubs and trees. Plants in this genus vary widely in size, ranging from 8m to as much as 25m tall, and from 3m–6m in width. *Cassia* is native to the tropics and subtropics of Africa, America, Asia, and Australia.

While the foliage of the various *Cassia* species varies in appearance, all feature bi-pinnate leaves. These trees also share a common flower type, bearing showy yellow or golden five-petalled, bowl-shaped blooms. While these flowers are occasionally single, they are usually borne in panicles or racemes. *Cassia* is particularly attractive as a specimen plant or in a shrub border, as it flowers throughout the year.

The following are the most common *Cassia* species grown in the Arabian Gulf region:

***Cassia fistula*, golden shower tree:** The golden shower tree is the national tree of Thailand, and is considered one of the most beautiful of all the tropical trees. This spreading, semi-evergreen to deciduous tree grows to a height of 8–12m, and spreads to a width of 3–5m. The foliage of *Cassia fistula* is composed of long, bi-pinnate, bright green leaves, each about 60cm in length, made up of 6–16 ovate leaflets. Amid the leaves bloom fragrant, bright yellow flowers, five-petalled, each 4–7cm in diameter and of equal size and shape. These prominent blossoms emerge in pendent racemes, 20–40cm long, beginning in May and lasting throughout the summer. As the season fades and the flowers wilt, long black cylindrical fruit pods appear. These fruit pods average about 30–60cm in length and 1.5–2.5cm in width. The legumes have a strong odor and contain brown seeds.

The fast-growing, drought tolerant golden shower tree is a popular choice for public planting in parks and on roadsides throughout Qatar and the Middle East. Although older trees will shed their leaves in winter or in times of drought, this tree is surprising resilient, and can thrive with little attention and in poor soil.

***Cassia javanica*, pink shower tree:** This many-branched, spreading tree can range from 12–25m in height and 3–6m wide. It features downy-textured young foliage, which matures into leaves that can measure up to 40cm long. Each bi-pinnate leaf is composed of 16–34 elliptic to oblong-elliptic leaflets. *Cassia javanica* flowers in May, and continues to bloom throughout the summer. The blossoms of the pink shower tree are pale pink, crimson, or buff-pink in color, and emerge in rigid racemes measuring 10cm or more in length.

Opposite page
Cassia fistula
Golden shower tree flowers

Care: *Cassia* trees are hardy, and can be pruned regularly to encourage a denser crown and a pleasing shape. During the growing season they should be watered regularly, and they require a monthly application of a balanced liquid fertilizer. *Cassia* can be planted in any area of the garden that is dry and receives full sun all day.

Propagation: Although plants in the *Cassia* genus can be propagated by seed in many parts of the world, this method is not viable in the Arabian Gulf region, as the seeds will not mature. In areas where *Cassia* can be propagated by seed, the seeds should be soaked in warm water 24 hours before planting. In the Gulf region, *Cassia* trees can be propagated by grafting, using greenwood cuttings.

Pests and diseases: Members of the genus *Cassia* are susceptible to red spider mites and whiteflies, both of which should be treated by a licensed exterminator.

Uses: The fruit of the *Cassia* tree has medicinal benefits. The skin of the fruit, dried and ground into a powder, then mixed with saffron and rosewater, is given to women to speed up delivery once labor has begun. The pulp of this fruit is used medicinally in some regions as a purgative. The *Cassia* tree also has strong, durable wood, which can be used in construction.

Opposite page
Cassia fistula
Golden shower tree

Above
Cassia fistula
Golden shower tree
flowers, leaves and fruits

Opposite page
Cassia javanica
Pink shower tree flowers

Above
Cassia javanica
Pink shower tree,
leaves and trunk

Casuarina equisetifolia
Horsetail Tree

Native to Australia and the Pacific Islands, *Casuarina* is a genus of about 15 distinct species of perennial, evergreen plants. These conifer-like trees and shrubs, sometimes known as Australian pines, are cultivated for their foliage. Their leaves emerge as minute scales or teeth arranged in a collar-like ring at each branch node. *Casuarina* trees are grown as specimen plants, and may also be used by landscapers as windbreaks or ornamental trees along streets and seashores.

***Casuarina equisetifolia*, horsetail tree, ironwood:** An open, erect to spreading plant, the horsetail tree has a straight, cylindrical and usually branchless trunk covered in light greyish-brown bark. The trunk is smooth when the tree is young, becoming rough, thick, and furrowed as the tree matures, flaking into oblong pieces on older trees and showing an inner bark that is reddish or deep brown. Horsetail trees reach an average height of between 5 and 15m, though some stretch as high as 25–35m. The trunk usually measures 100–150cm in diameter, and most trees spread 3–8m in width. *Casuarina equisetifolia* often grow 1–3m per year, and some trees have been known to reach 9m in two years. These majestic trees are supported by a dense, spreading, fibrous root system.

Casuarina equisetifolia have pendent, long, thin-jointed, grey-green branches sporting foliage composed of insignificant leaves, making them pine-like or needle-like in appearance. Each leaf is only 1mm long, and leaves are arranged in whorls of six to eight. Unlike most other members of the *Casuarina* genus, *Casuarina equisetifolia* is a monoecious tree, with male and female flowers produced on the same plant. The flowers are borne in small, catkin-like inflorescences in spring. Male blossoms emerge in simple, cylindrical spikes measuring 4–7cm in length, positioned at the tips of the leaf twigs. The tiny, brownish-red female flowers grow in short peduncles on the branchlets below the leaf twigs.

Horsetail tree blossoms are pollinated by the wind, and female cones mature about 18–20 weeks after pollination. This tree produces fruit in the form of oval, woody structures, 10–24mm long and 9–13mm in diameter. The fruits are cone-like, although these plants are not conifers. Each fruit is grey or yellow-brown in color, and contains between 70 and 90 winged seeds.

Opposite page
Casuarina equisetifolia
Horsetail tree flowers

Above
Casuarina equisetifolia
Horsetail tree fruits

Caution: *Casuarina* pollen may cause allergic reactions including respiratory problems, eye irritation, rhinitis, and/or hoarseness.

Care: *Casuarina* trees flourish in locations where they can receive full sun all day. They make great additions to Gulf gardens as they can withstand strong winds, are salt-tolerant, and can grow in wet or dry soil. They require little special care, aside from ample water and applications of a balanced liquid fertilizer monthly during the growing season. These trees are hardy, and can be pruned regularly to maintain a pleasant shape and encourage a denser crown.

Propagation: Trees in the *Casuarina* genus can be propagated from seed in springtime; plants begin producing seeds when they are only three to five years old. *Casuarina equisetifolia* can also be propagated from semi-ripe cuttings in mid- or late summer.

Pests and diseases: Trees in the *Casuarina* genus are not commonly susceptible to pests or diseases.

Uses: *Casuarina equisetifolia* gets one of its common names, ironwood, from the very hard quality wood the plant produces. This heavy, dark, red-brown wood is used for building boats, electric poles, fences, furniture, gates, house posts, mine props, oars, pilings, rafters, roofing shingles, tool handles, wagon wheels, yokes, and fencing. Due to its rapid growth pattern, it is a source of fine quality fuel wood, and this is its main commercial use today, especially in Asia and Africa.

Casuarina trees have uses beyond their wood production. The pulp has been used to make paper, and extracts from the bark are used for tanning hides and staining and preserving fishing lines and fabrics. Wood ash is an ingredient in some soaps, and the cone-like structures of the tree are used in novelties for the tourist trade. Medicinally, a decoction from the astringent bark of *Casuarina* trees has been used as a remedy for diarrhea, sore throat, cough, headache, toothache, sores, and swellings.

Various *Casuarina* species serve different landscaping purposes. *Casuarina oligodon* is planted as a cover crop for coffee. Trees in the *Casuarina* genus are known for fixing nitrogen into the soil, and as such are planted among crops such as coconuts. *Casuarina* trees are also widely used as bonsai subjects.

Opposite page
Casuarina equisetifolia
Horsetail tree

Ceiba
Silk Cotton Tree

Native to Africa and Asia, as well as Brazil and Argentina, *Ceiba* is a genus of 22 distinct species of large, spiny-trunked, semi-evergreen or deciduous trees. Some of these unique trees maintain a relatively narrow crown with one straight trunk, while other, particularly older, trees are wide-spreading. Growing to a mature height of 15–70m, and spreading to an equal or greater diameter, these succulent plants have spiny, very fleshy trunks. *Ceiba* trees produce large, showy, pink and white, five-petalled flowers. They are resistant to drought and tolerate moderately cold temperatures.

The following are the most common *Ceiba* species grown in the Arabian Gulf region:

***Ceiba pentandra*, kapok, white silk cotton tree:** The kapok is a large, deciduous, tropical tree. Erect when young, *Ceiba pentandra* spreads to an eventual width of 5–25m. Reaching a final height of 25–70m, with a trunk up to 3m in diameter, this tree changes in appearance as it matures. The trunk and branches of some juvenile trees are covered with heavy conical spines on brown or silvery bark, while others are mostly spineless with silver or green bark. Older trees become more uniform in shape, with straight, cylindrical, grey trunks. Those trees with spines lose most or all of them with age. *Ceiba pentandra* trees have branches that grow in horizontal tiers, and spread widely. Older kapok trees can be identified by their very large buttresses and surface roots. These lend greater stability to the tree's massive trunk.

Kapok trees feature foliage consisting of alternate, palmate, mid-green leaves, each about 8–15cm long. Each leaf is composed of five to seven oblong lance-shaped, entire leaflets with short stalks. The tree sheds its leaves as it prepares to bloom. *Ceiba pentandra* are hermaphrodite, producing flowers that contain both male and female reproductive parts. This tree flowers from late winter to early spring, with dense, pendent, axillary clusters of cup-shaped, yellow, white, or pink five-petalled blossoms emerging near the end of the tree's branches. Each small, fragrant flower measures 6cm across, with brown hairs on its surface. The blooms are borne on bare stems and open only in the evening.

Bats, birds and bees are the major pollinators of the *Ceiba pentandra* tree, and woody seed capsules mature in spring and summer. Each capsule is 10–30cm long, oblong or elliptic in shape and tapering off at the ends, containing 120–175 rounded black-brown seeds embedded in a mass of grey woolly hairs (known as floss). The mature capsules split into five segments releasing the characteristic "silk cotton." Each segment is 1.5–3cm long, and is covered with a waxy substance, making the floss water-repellent. White silk cotton trees are cultivated for this seed fiber.

***Ceiba speciosa* (synonym *Chorisia speciosa*), silk cotton tree:** Unique and eye-catching from its trunk to its flowers, the silk cotton tree is considered by some to be one of the most beautiful trees in the world. Its striking appearance and large size make it an excellent specimen tree. *Ceiba speciosa* is a deciduous tree, generally conical in shape, developing a rounded, umbrella-like crown as it matures. Silk cotton trees grow rapidly when they are young,

Opposite page
Ceiba speciosa
Silk cotton tree flower

Above
Ceiba speciosa
Silk cotton tree

as much as 5m per year, and also experience spurts of growth when water is abundant. Sapling silk cotton trees have a green trunk, containing high levels of chlorophyll, which allows photosynthesis even in the absence of leaves. The trunk gradually turns grey as the tree ages. The tree's long, bottle-shaped trunk usually bulges towards the base, measuring as much as 2m in diameter. It is studded with thick conical prickles, which serve to store water in preparation for drought.

The branches of the silk cotton tree emerge horizontally from the trunk. Like the trunk, they are green when the tree is young, gradually fading to grey as it matures. Also like the trunk, the branches are covered in prickles. From the branches grow alternate palmate leaves, each about 12cm long, composed of five to seven lance-shaped, often toothed leaflets. Leaves fall from the tree as it prepares to bloom.

From October to November and December, the silk cotton tree produces dramatic, hibiscus-like flowers. These five-petalled, funnel-shaped blossoms, creamy white in the center and pink towards the petal tips, can measure 10–15cm in diameter or more, and bloom singly from the leaf axils. The flowers produce a nectar that attracts butterflies to the tree, enabling pollination.

Ceiba speciosa bears large, pear-shaped fruit, initially green in color, then ripening to shades of brown. These oblong pods, measuring about

Above
Ceiba speciosa
Silk cotton tree flowers, fruit, trunk and leaves

Right
Ceiba pentandra
White silk cotton tree

20cm in length, hold black, pea-like seeds encased by silk-like fibers, which is where the tree gets its common name.

Care: *Ceiba* trees thrive in full sun, perfect for the Gulf region, although they do require some specialized care. Plant trees in moist, well-drained soil. Water moderately during the growing season, tapering off during the dormant months, and apply liquid fertilizer two to three times per year. Prune the tips of branches to encourage new growth and more frequent flowering.

Propagation: From seed. *Ceiba* trees can also be propagated by rooting semi-ripe cuttings.

Pests and diseases: Young *Ceiba* trees are particularly susceptible to scale insect damage. These pests should be treated by a licensed exterminator.

Uses: Fiber from the seed capsules of the *Ceiba pentandra* tree is light, buoyant, resilient, and water resistant. It was previously used as filling for life jackets, and is still used today as an alternative to down as a filling in mattresses, pillows, upholstery, sofas, and stuffed toys. It is also used in buildings as insulation.

Aside from the plant's "silk cotton" fibers, many other parts of the tree are also useful. The seeds of the kapok tree produce an oil that is used in making soap, and can be used as fertilizer. In West Africa, the seeds are eaten roasted or in soups. The flowers are an important source of nectar and pollen for honey bees, and the leaves serve as fodder for cattle, goats, and sheep. Medicinally, the seeds, leaves, bark, and resin of *Ceiba pentandra* have been used to treat dysentery, fever, asthma, and kidney disease. Finally, because of its size, the kapok tree is sometimes planted as a shade tree for crops such as coffee and tea.

In addition to being very beautiful, most parts of the *Ceiba speciosa* tree are useful. Wood made from the trunk of silk floss trees is light, soft, and flexible. It is used for building canoes. The wood's pulp can be made into paper. The bark of this tree, cut into strips, has been used to make rope. The petals of its flowers can be woven into upholstery. Although the fruits of the silk cotton tree are inedible, they are still valuable. The cotton-like fibers inside the fruit pods are used as stuffing for a variety of objects including pillows, upholstery, and softballs, and as a packing material. The seeds of the fruit produce an oil that is edible, and also has industrial uses.

Above
Ceiba pentandra
White silk cotton tree fruits at various stages of growth

Cerbera manghas
Sea Mango

Cerbera, a genus of six to eight species of evergreen trees and shrubs, is native to tropical Asia, Australia, Madagascar, the Seychelles, and islands in the western Pacific Ocean. Plants in this genus tend to be small trees or shrubs, and some varieties in this group are mangroves.

Cerbera manghas, sea mango: *Cerbera manghas*, commonly known as sea mango, is an evergreen tree that thrives in coastal regions. Ranging from 6–15m in height, this tree has a glabrous trunk which averages 70cm in diameter. The trunk is covered in thick, rough, flaky grey- to brown-hued bark, and will emit a white latex substance when scarred or cut. Emerging from the trunk are thick, succulent branches, often bearing scars from fallen leaves. *Cerbera manghas* has foliage consisting of spirally arranged leaves, borne on green or yellow stems, clustered at the ends of its branches. Its glossy, dark green leaves are alternate, simple and entire, and ovoid or lanceolate to oblong-lanceolate in shape. Each leaf, narrowed and pointed at both ends, measures 13–25cm long and is pinnately veined, with 15–40 pairs of lateral veins.

Sea mangoes flower from April through August, producing terminal inflorescences of bright, fragrant blossoms. Each greenish-white bloom has a short calyx tube, about 2cm long, five broadly spreading lobed corolla, and a contrasting hairy center that may be pink, red, white, purple or yellowish in color. Flowers measure 3–5cm in diameter, have five stamens, and have an ovary which is positioned well above the other parts of the bloom. The blossoms of *Cerbera manghas* are pollinated by insects. After pollination, this tree produces fruits in the form of ovoid or egg-shaped drupes, 5–10cm long, which are flattened on one side. The fruits are fibrous and woody on the inside and initially green outside, maturing to a bright red and ripening to a rosy purple, then eventually turning black. Each fruit contains only one oily seed, and fresh fruits exude a milky substance when cut.

Sea mango trees are usually planted in the garden as ornamental specimens. It must be noted, however, that these trees are considered one of the 10 most toxic plants in the tropical region. All parts of the *Cerbera manghas* tree contain cerberia, a cardiac glycoside, which is a substance that blocks electric impulses in the body (including the beating of the heart). This substance is so toxic that the wood of this tree should not be used in fires, as the smoke may cause poisoning.

Caution: The leaves, flowers, fruit, and white latex substance exuded by this plant when cut are all extremely poisonous.

Care: Sea mango trees thrive in sunny locations. They require fertile, humus-rich, moist yet well-drained soil. These trees should be watered moderately during the growing season, and less frequently throughout the plant's dormant months.

Propagation: Sea mangoes can be propagated by seed. To harvest the seeds, either remove the pulp of fresh fruits, or dry the fruits and then crack open to remove the seeds.

Pests and diseases: *Cerbera manghas* are susceptible to mealy bug damage. These pests should be treated by a licensed exterminator.

Opposite page
Cerbera manghas
Sea mango flower

Above
Cerbera manghas
Sea mango

Uses: Various parts of the sea mango tree are used for a wide range of purposes. Industrially, the wood of this tree is occasionally used in tropical Asia in building construction for moldings, interior trim, core veneer, and shuttering. It is also used to produce clogs, plain furniture, and crates for fruit. The dried, fibrous fruits of this plant are sometimes used in flower arrangements. In the Philippines, the poison sap from the bark of this tree is used by local fishermen fishing in small ponds or streams.

Medicinally, many parts of the *Cerbera manghas* plant are effective in treating a variety of ailments. Oil from the seeds of this tree can be used in poultices applied to the skin to treat scabies and prurigo. This oil can also be applied to the hair and scalp to treat head lice. Glycosides extracted from the seeds are an ingredient used in the treatment of congestive heart failure. The bark and the leaves of the sea mango have purgative and antipyretic properties, and are used in the treatment of dysuria and ringworm. They are highly toxic, however, and precautions should be taken with their consumption. Sea mango flowers can be used to treat hemorrhoids, and the pulp of the fresh fruit of this tree can be rubbed on the legs to sooth the pain of rheumatism. The pulp of this fruit, when combined with the herb *Datura*, can be used to treat hydrophobia, and the kernel of this fruit has been used in traditional medicine as an abortifacient.

Above
Cerbera manghas
Sea mango flowers, fruits and leaves

Coccoloba uvifera
Sea Grape

Coccoloba is a genus of about 120–150 species of shrubs and trees. Native to Mexico, Central America, and the Caribbean, these flowering, predominantly evergreen plants are grown today in coastal areas throughout the tropics and subtropics.

***Coccoloba uvifera*, sea grape:** In its native habitat, *Coccoloba uvifera* is a large shrub or more often a small tree. Commonly known as the sea grape, these trees range from 8–17m in height. Although in cultivation they are usually seen as medium-sized shrubs, with age these plants can grow into large, multi-stemmed trees. The trunks of the sea grape are smooth and covered in peeling bark that is mottled white, grey, and light brown in color. If the bark is scored, the tree produces an astringent, tannin-rich, red sap.

Coccoloba uvifera features showy foliage consisting of large, alternate, simple, leathery leaves, 20cm in diameter and 25cm in length. Each leaf is rounded, with a heart-shaped base, a rounded leaf apex and an entire margin. New foliage is usually bronze in color, maturing to a bright green with red veins. At the end of the season, aged leaves will turn completely red, before being shed in the winter.

In addition to their attractive foliage, sea grapes produce slender, terminal and lateral spikes of flowers, each 15.2–25.4cm long. These spikes protrude beyond the length of the leaves, bearing tiny, fragrant white flowers. Each blossom is composed of a calyx with five green sepals and a corolla with five whitish petals, one pistil, and eight white stamens.

Coccoloba uvifera is dioecious, meaning that plants are actually male or female, depending on the type of flowers they produce. Cross-pollination is necessary for fruits to develop; insects and honey bees carry out this process.

Sea grapes get their common name from the edible, round, grape-like fruit or drupes they produce. Borne in pendant clusters, these tiny fruits are initially green, ripening to purple-red, and approximately 1.9–2cm in diameter. Emerging in late summer, each small drupe has a thin layer of flesh surrounding a large hard pit.

Sea grapes are hardy trees, able to thrive in salty soil and to tolerate strong sun and high winds. This makes them a viable addition to gardens in the Gulf region, as well as a popular landscaping choice in coastal regions everywhere. These trees are often grown as windbreaks near beaches, and make great hedges or shrub borders. Although sea grape trees usually have branches that are stout and low to the ground, if grown away from strong, salty winds they can develop into lovely vase-shaped trees. In this form sea grapes can be used as street trees, or as shade trees in gardens or parks. Sea grapes attract birds, and add a nice tropical feel to any landscape.

Caution: *Coccoloba uvifera* pollen can cause significant allergy symptoms.

Care: *Coccoloba uvifera* trees are outdoor plants, thriving in locations that receive partial to full sunlight. Although drought tolerant, young sea grape trees should be watered regularly until they are well-established. These trees require regular pruning to maintain a neat canopy, and to encourage the trees' multiple trunks to develop a strong structure.

Opposite page
Coccoloba uvifera
Sea grape leaves

Propagation: From seed. Freshly collected seeds must be sown immediately, and cannot be stored for future use. Germination typically occurs within 18–50 days. *Coccoloba uvifera* can also be propagated from cuttings, or by ground-layering.

Pests and diseases: *Coccoloba uvifera* trees are susceptible to mite, mealy bug and scale insect damage. All of these pests should be treated by a licensed exterminator.

Uses: Sea grape is a versatile, extremely useful tree. For landscaping purposes, sea grapes are often planted to make a light barrier along coastlines to protect sea turtles. Wood from the trunks of larger trees is prized for cabinet work and boats, and smaller trunks and branches can be made into charcoal and used for firewood. In the West Indies, sea grape wood is boiled to extract a red dye, used for staining and tanning leather. Bees collect pollen from sea grape flowers, which they make into a pale, spicy-flavored honey. Fresh sea grape fruits are edible, and can be made into jams, jellies, and wine. They can also be used to produce vinegar.

Medicinally, various parts of the sea grape plant can be boiled together to make a tea, which can be used to treat diarrhea. Gum from the bark of the tree can be taken for throat ailments, and the roots of this tree are used in traditional medicine to treat dysentery. Externally, sea grape leaves can be made into a compress which can be applied to boils, or as a poultice used to treat headaches.

Opposite page
Coccoloba uvifera
Sea grape

Above
Coccoloba uvifera
Sea grape flowers and fruits

Cochlospermum religiosum
Buttercup Tree, Yellow Silk Cotton Tree

Cochlospermum is a small genus of 12–15 species of deciduous shrubs and trees. Native to Mexico, Venezuela, India, Burma, Thailand, and Australia, these perennials range in height from 7–12m.

***Cochlospermum religiosum,* yellow silk cotton tree, buttercup tree:** The buttercup tree, so named for its golden-yellow flowers, is an open, spreading tree. Reaching a mature height of between 7.5 and 10m, it has a trunk covered in smooth, pale or dark grey, fibrous bark. This bark, when cut, exudes a substance called gum. From the branches emerge alternate, palmately rounded, deeply three to five lobed or pinnatifid, long-stalked, mid- to dark green leaves. Each leaf may reach a width of 30cm, and has elliptic to narrowly obovate, entire or crenate-margined lobes. The "buttercup" blossoms of this tree are bowl-shaped, large, five-petalled flowers, 10–12cm in diameter, yellow in hue with scarlet and orange stamens. They bloom in terminal panicles, 15–30cm long, in winter through early summer. Once the flowers have faded large, capsule-shaped fruits emerge. Each fruit has five leathery brown segments, which eventually split open to release black, curved seeds. These seeds are about 6mm long, and are covered in white, silky cotton hairs. It is from these hairs that the tree gets its other common name, yellow silk cotton tree.

Care: Yellow silk cotton trees make lovely specimen plants. Grown outdoors, they should be planted in moderately fertile, well-drained soil, and placed in full sun. This tree requires regular pruning to maintain a balanced shape. The optimal pruning time is when the tree is leafless, or immediately after flowering.

Propagation: From seed or by layering in the summertime. Buttercup trees can also be propagated by rooting greenwood or semi-ripe cuttings.

Pests and diseases: Trees in the *Cochlospermum* genus are susceptible to red spider mite damage. These pests should only be treated by a licensed exterminator.

Uses: Every part of the buttercup tree is useful. The bark of the tree contains fibers that can be used to make rope. Also, when ground into a fine powder, the bark has medicinal properties, and can be mixed with water and taken orally as a treatment for jaundice. The leaves and flowers of this plant, when dried, are given as a treatment for asthma and mouth

Opposite page
Cochlospermum religiosum
Yellow silk cotton
tree flower

Right
Cochlospermum religiosum
Yellow silk cotton tree

ulcers, as well as having stimulant properties. Buttercup tree seeds have a non-drying oil that is used in soaps. The seed-cake that is a by-product of the oil removal process can be fed to cattle, and is also a natural fertilizer. The silky cotton fibers that surround the seeds in their pods are believed to induce sleep when stuffed into pillows.

The most useful part of this tree, however, is the gum excreted from the bark. Katira gum swells in water, and does not dissolve. This gum is very valuable, and serves a wide variety of purposes. Industrially, it can be used as a waterborne adhesive paste, and is a substitute for gum tragacanth in various industrial processes. It is an ingredient in calico printing and paper making, and in India is used for curing leather. The gum is used in the making of cigars and ice-cream, and even has medicinal properties. It has a mildly sweet flavor, and its cooling and sedative effects make it useful in the treatment of a wide range of ailments including cough, diarrhea, dysentery, pharyngitis, gonorrhea, syphilis and trachoma.

Above
Cochlospermum religiosum
Yellow silk cotton tree flower, fruits and leaves

Conocarpus lancifolius
Damas Tree

Conocarpus is a small genus of only two distinct species of flowering, evergreen trees. Ranging in height from 1m to as much as 20m, this genus includes dense, multiple-trunked shrubs, as well as small to medium-sized trees.

Conocarpus lancifolius, damas tree: Native to northeast Africa and the southwest Arabian Peninsula, but planted over a much wider area, *Conocarpus lancifolius*, commonly known as the damas tree, is a fast-growing evergreen. This large shrub or small tree reaches a mature height of 6.5–14m. Although it is an attractive ornamental tree, these plants develop long, deep root systems, and these roots can effect nearby plants and even destroy the foundation of buildings. For this reason, they are best planted alone, with an open area surrounding them. Damas trees are perfect for large gardens or public parks, and can also be grown along roadsides or in desert areas.

Conocarpus lancifolius has full, deep green foliage. Its leaves are narrow or lance-shaped, and measure 15–20cm in length. In springtime this tree produces small, creamy white flowers followed by red, pepper-like fruit. *Conocarpus lancifolius* thrives when planted in soil that is fortified with organic material.

Opposite page
Conocarpus lancifolius
Damas tree fruits

Above
Conocarpus lancifolius
Damas tree

The growth patterns of *Conocarpus lancifolius* trees are easily controlled by pruning. How a gardener chooses to use the tree often determines how it is trained to grow. If planted as a specimen tree, then saplings should be planted at least 4–5m apart. Once the tree is established, branches are pruned so that the tree grows vertically, instead of spreading. Trained in this manner, the tree will attain maximum height. If the purpose of the planting is to establish a windbreak, saplings should be placed close together, approximately every 100–150cm. To make a hedge or natural privacy fence, to surround a property or partition a garden, plant young trees even closer together, leaving a distance of only 75–100cm. Once the trees are established, prune from the top rather than the sides, allowing the lower branches to grow and spread.

Care: For best results, *Conocarpus lancifolius* should be placed in a location receiving full sun all day, and planted in moderately fertile, well-drained soil fortified with organic material. These trees make beautiful specimen plants; they do, however, require regular pruning to maintain a balanced shape.

Propagation: From seed. *Conocarpus lancifolius* can also be propagated using cuttings in the wintertime, from November to February. Cuttings should be taken as new shoots, or cut from a green branch. The cutting, which should be about 15cm in length, is then placed in either liquid or powder rooting hormone prior to placing in compost. Cuttings remain in the rooting medium until they begin to grow roots. At this stage the cuttings are placed in small (5cm) pots filled with peat moss, or a mixture of 40% peat moss, 40% sand and 20% pearlite. Water the cuttings, cover the pots with film, and wait until small leaves form. Once leaves have sprouted, the new plants can be placed in the garden.

Pests and diseases: *Conocarpus lancifolius* is not commonly susceptible to pests or diseases.

Uses: Damas trees are hardy plants, tolerant to drought and salty soil, and as such make excellent windbreaks for gardens and farms in this region. Their wood is useful as charcoal, and their leaves are sometimes added to cattle feed.

Opposite page
Conocarpus lancifolius
Damas tree

Above
Conocarpus lancifolius
Damas tree leaves

Cordia
Orange Cordia, White Cordia

A native of the tropics and subtropics, *Cordia* is a genus consisting of about 300 species of evergreen and deciduous, small trees and shrubs.

The following are the most common *Cordia* species grown in the Arabian Gulf region:

Cordia boissieri, white cordia, Texas wild olive: Native to Mexico and spreading north into the southern US state of Texas, this small tree reaches a maximum height of 5–7m, and sports a symmetrically round crown 3–5m wide. The white cordia has foliage consisting of alternate, simple, large, rough textured, ovate leaves. Each leaf is grey-green above and paler below, 9–18cm long and 5–9cm wide. These leaves serve as a backdrop for the tree's funnel-shaped, white flowers. Each small blossom, 3–5cm in diameter, has a yellow center and a crepe paper texture. *Cordia boissieri* blooms year-round, with peak bloom occurring from spring into summer.

This tree takes its other common name, Texas wild olive, from its olive-like, fleshy round fruit. These inedible fruit are 1–2.5cm in length, large, with a single seed. They are sweet but slightly toxic when fresh, causing dizziness if consumed by humans or animals.

Cordia boissieri are often planted as ornamental trees, because of their compact size and showy, year-round flowers, and can even be planted in an above-ground container. They may be used as specimen trees or as an accent in a border, and their fruit and flowers will attract butterflies and hummingbirds to the garden. White cordia trees have an average lifespan of 30–50 years.

***Cordia sebestena*, orange cordia, geiger tree:** The orange cordia, when mature, is a beautiful round-headed, multi-trunk tree. As a sapling, however, it has a vaguely pyramidal shape, and takes about five years to develop a dense canopy. Its large, rough

Opposite page
Cordia boissieri
White cordia flowers

Above
Cordia boissieri
White cordia

Above
Cordia sebestena
Orange cordia

textured, oval to heart-shaped leaves are the perfect backdrop for its bright red and orange flowers. These colorful blossoms, with short yellow-orange stamens in the throat, bloom throughout the year, reaching a pinnacle in June and July. The blossoms, which are about 10cm in diameter, give way to berry-like fruit. This fruit is edible, though not particularly tasty. Reaching a maximum height of 3–7m, the orange cordia can be used as a specimen or accent tree, particularly when planted at the corner or entry of a house.

Care: Although an attractive facet of any garden, trees in the *Cordia* genus tend to be messy, shedding their leaves year-round. Also, these trees must be staked when they are young to guide trunk growth, and they require regular pruning to establish and maintain a balanced shape. Fertilize *Cordia* trees once or twice a year, to ensure full growth and maximum flowering.

Propagation: From seed, cuttings, or by air-layering. *Cordia* saplings will not flower until they are at least three years old.

Pests and diseases: Trees in the *Cordia* genus are susceptible to red spider mite, scale insect, and caterpillar damage, all of which should be treated by a licensed exterminator.

Uses: *Cordia boissieri* is a useful member of the *Cordia* genus. The wood of this tree is used as firewood and for carpentry. A syrup made from the fruits of the white cordia is used to dye cloth, and jellies made from the fruits are reportedly safe to eat. Syrup made from the fruit is used medicinally to treat coughs, and the leaves are used to alleviate symptoms of rheumatism and pulmonary illness.

Above
Cordia sebestena
Orange cordia leaf, fruit and flowers

Cupressus
Cypress

Cupressus, a genus of 25 species of coniferous trees, is native to the temperate regions of North America, Europe, North Africa, and central and eastern Asia. These tall, stately trees, ranging from 10 to 35m in height, are evergreen perennials.

Cupressus trees, commonly known as cypress, feature foliage composed of pairs of overlapping, scale-like leaves. These leaves are forward-pointing, and can be either rounded or pointed at the tips. Cypress trees are monoecious, producing both male and female cones. Male cones are small, only 2–3mm long, green in color, and erupt from the tips of the tree's shoots. Female cones are more spherical in shape, growing as long as 4cm, and have 5–20 seeds per scale. These cones ripen during the tree's second year of growth, but usually remain on the tree. As it matures, the bark of the cypress tree often breaks off into curled or rounded scales.

Cypress trees are hardy and tolerate dry conditions, and as such can be versatile additions to any garden. They make excellent specimen trees, and may be planted singly in containers. They can also be planted in groups, spaced 2–3m apart, to form a hedge or privacy fence around a property.

The following are the most common *Cupressus* species grown in the Arabian Gulf region:

Cupressus macrocarpa, Monterey cypress: The Monterey cypress, a mid-size member of the *Cupressus* group, reaches a maximum height of about 30–35m, and a width of 4–12m. When young, this tree is pyramidal in shape, but as it grows its dome broadens and it develops a narrowly conical to columnar profile in maturity. *Cupressus macrocarpa* features a trunk which is covered with shallowly ridged, scaly reddish-brown bark, and from which grows its numerous branches. The Monterey cypress has foliage composed of pointed, bright green, lemon-scented leaves. The leaves are arranged in opposite, adjacent pairs at right-angles, each about 2mm long, that grow in erect or spreading, plume-like sprays. Monterey cypress trees produce spherical brown female cones, each about 2–3cm across, with eight to 18 scales that lack a prominent prickle,

Opposite page and above
Cupressus macrocarpa
Monterey cypress

Right
Cupressus sempervirens
Italian cypress

as well as male cones, which are 3–5mm in diameter, yellow, and carried on the lower parts of shoots. This tree has a spiky-topped appearance when young, and can be planted in a container, surrounded by annual flowers. The tree spreads wide with age, however, and will eventually need to be transplanted to a permanent place in the garden, where it will serve as a natural windbreak.

Cupressus sempervirens, Italian cypress: Italian cypress are majestic, towering trees, narrowly conical, columnar or rarely spreading, reaching an eventual height of 20–30m and a width of 1m to as much as 6m. Their foliage consists of horizontal branches bearing dense sprays of grey-green or dark green, glandless leaves. Each leaf is about 1mm long, usually with rounded, pointed tips on strong shoots. This conifer produces spherical to ovoid, prickly brown female cones, about 2–3cm long, with eight to 14 scales. Italian cypress establish themselves quickly; they do not, however, mature for 15–20 years after planting.

Care: *Cupressus* trees are a popular choice for Middle East gardens, as they thrive in full sun. Plant trees in well-drained soil. For *Cupressus* specimens that are planted as hedges, trim plants in late spring.

Propagation: From seed. *Cupressus* trees can also be propagated by rooting semi-ripe cuttings.

Pests and diseases: Trees in the *Cupressus* genus are susceptible to cypress aphid, and are prone to infestation by fungal pathogens such as *Phytophthora* and coryneum canker. These conditions should be treated by an experienced gardener or a licensed exterminator.

Uses: All parts of the *Cupressus* tree are useful for a variety of domestic and medicinal purposes. Smoke from burning cypress wood is a natural insecticide, particularly effective against bed bugs and chinch bugs. Crushed cypress leaves can be made into a poultice, which can be applied to wounds to speed healing or to the chest to treat coughs and chest pain. Leaves and pine cones from cypress trees excrete a fragrant oil, which is used in making soap, household cleaners, and room deodorizers. Medicinally, this oil can be used in the treatment of hemorrhoids and varicose veins. Small pine cones can be placed into warm water to create a soothing footbath. The fruit of the cypress tree, crushed into a powder, can be mixed with water to make a gargle. This gargle can be taken to ease toothaches and gum inflammation.

Above
Cupressus sempervirens
Italian cypress
fruit and leaves

Dalbergia sissoo
Indian Rosewood, Sisu, Sheesham

Native to the tropical regions of Central and South America, Africa, Madagascar, and southern Asia, *Dalbergia* is a large genus of approximately 594 evergreens. These medium to large deciduous perennials include both trees and shrubs. Many species in the *Dalbergia* genus are important timber trees. They are valued for their decorative and often fragrant wood, which is rich in oils.

***Dalbergia sissoo*, Indian rosewood, sisu, sheesham:** Native to the Indian Subcontinent and Southern Iran, *Dalbergia sissoo* is the most famous of the rosewood species. The state tree of the Punjab region of India, this medium to large deciduous or semi-evergreen tree has an open, spreading crown, and grows to a height of 12–35m. *Dalbergia sissoo* has a long taproot and numerous surface roots which produce suckers. Its trunk, measuring 2–3m in diameter, is often crooked, and covered in bark that is light brown to dark grey. This bark may be as much as 2.5cm thick, and sheds in narrow strips.

Indian rosewoods feature foliage consisting of alternate, compound, oddly pinnate leaves, with three to five leathery, light to medium green ovate to orbicular leaflets. Each leaf is about 15cm long. In spring, *Dalbergia sissoo* produces dense terminal racemes of whitish to pink or dull yellow blossoms. Each raceme is 5–10cm long, and the tiny, fragrant, nearly sessile blooms are 1.5cm long. These flowers are followed by oblong, flat, thin, light brown, strap-like pods, 4–8cm long and 1cm wide. Each pod contains between one and five flat, bean-shaped seeds measuring 8–10mm in length. Mature seed pods remain on the tree for seven to eight months.

Dalbergia sissoo trees are used in landscaping as natural windbreaks, as well as in parks for shade, and as street trees. Once established, they reach maturity at 19–21 years of age, and can live as long as 60 years. Indian rosewoods are highly valued for their fragrant flowers, and are often used in gardens as ornamental trees. *Dalbergia sissoo* has been introduced in various countries throughout the world, although it has been classified as an invasive species in Australia and in the southern US state of Florida.

Care: *Dalbergia sissoo* trees are outdoor plants, and should be placed in a location receiving full sun. These trees require fertile, moist but well-drained soil, enhanced by a monthly application of a balanced liquid fertilizer. Indian rosewoods should be watered freely during the growing season. This tree needs regular pruning to maintain a balanced shape.

Propagation: Indian rosewood can be propagated from seed in springtime. Seeds should be soaked in warm water for at least 48 hours before planting, and will germinate in one to three weeks. This tree can also be propagated by cutting or by root suckers.

Pests and diseases: Indian rosewoods are not typically susceptible to pests and diseases. However, several species of fungi, insects, and bacteria may cause mortality or stunt the growth of the tree.

Uses: Parts and products of the *Dalbergia sissoo* tree are useful industrially, agriculturally, medicinally, and cosmetically. The tree is primarily used for its high quality wood. This

Opposite page
Dalbergia sissoo
Indian rosewood

strong, tough timber is used to make furniture, plywood, bridge piles, sporting goods, railway sleepers, and musical instruments. Indian rosewood is also used as fuel wood and charcoal. Wood fibers are processed into a pulp that is further made into paper, and a non-drying fixed oil is processed from the wood and used as a lubricant in heavy machinery.

Agriculturally, this tree is planted in India among tea, mango, and coffee plants to provide shade for crops. *Dalbergia sissoo* contributes to erosion control and soil fertility wherever it is placed, because it is a member of the legume family and can fix nitrogen from the atmosphere through bacteria nodules on its root system. Also, leaf litter that accumulates and decomposes contributes to soil fertility by adding additional nitrogen, potassium, iron, manganese, and organic carbon to the ground. In some areas, the young branches and foliage of Indian rosewood are used as livestock fodder.

Medicinally, Indian rosewood is used in traditional remedies for a variety of ailments including skin diseases, blood diseases, syphilis, stomach problems, dysentery, nausea, and eye and nose disorders. The leaves can be pressed, and the resulting liquid mixed with honey. This combination can be used to treat conjunctivitis, and can also be taken to relieve indigestion.

Cosmetically, rosewood oil has been shown to stimulate skin cell renewal, and as such is used in anti-wrinkle and acne treatments. It is also an ingredient in some perfumes. In Punjab, the leaves are applied topically to whiten the skin, and to remove brown discoloring on the face.

Opposite page
Dalbergia sissoo
Indian rosewood fruits

Above
Dalbergia sissoo
Indian rosewood trunk

Delonix regia
Royal Poinciana, Flamboyant

Native to tropical Africa, *Delonix* is a genus of 11 species of semi-deciduous trees. These dramatic trees grow to a height of about 10m, and spread 5–10m in width.

Delonix regia (synonym Poinciana regia), royal poinciana, flame tree: The royal poinciana, originally from the island of Madagascar, quickly spread throughout the tropics, and is now one of the most popular ornamental trees in the world. Also known as the flame tree, it probably gets this colloquial name from its flame-red blossoms, which also come in hues of crimson, scarlet, orange, apricot, and even pale yellow with red stripes. This rapidly growing tree, when mature, features a dome of long, sweeping branches with attractive, bi-pinnate, fern-like, bright green leaves. Each leaf is 30–50cm long, and each pinna is divided into 10–25 pairs of alternate leaflets. These leaves close together at night. While its foliage alone makes it an attractive tree, the royal poinciana has eye-catching blossoms, emerging in clusters, each with five petals, and measuring between 10–13cm in diameter. The flowering pattern of this tree is irregular, and in some years blooms may emerge on only one part of the tree. As the season progresses the flowers are replaced by heavy brown seed pods up to 60cm long that remain on the tree for several months. Each pod contains a multitude of large dark brown seeds.

Flame trees require several years of growth before their first flowering. The plant may experience some die off of foliage each April, although new leaves immediately emerge. This tree is best planted alone for maximum visual impact in the garden.

Care: *Delonix regia* thrives when planted in fertile, moist, well-drained soil in a location that gets full sun. During the growing season this tree should be watered freely, and should also receive a monthly application of a balanced liquid fertilizer. Trim royal poinciana trees regularly to retain a pleasing shape.

Propagation: From seed, or by rooting semi-ripe cuttings. Seeds should be soaked in warm water for at least 24 hours before planting.

Pests and diseases: Royal poinciana trees are susceptible to red spider mite and whitefly damage. These pests should be treated by a licensed exterminator.

Uses: The seed-plentiful fruits of the royal poinciana are used as musical instruments in the Caribbean, similar to maracas. The seeds themselves are high in protein, and are often used as feed for livestock.

Opposite page
Delonix regia
Flame tree flowers

Above
Delonix regia
Flame tree

Above left
Delonix regia
Flame tree trunk, fruits and flower

Above right
Delonix regia var. flava
Flame tree leaves and flowers

Right
Delonix regia var. flava
(Flame tree with apricot flowers)

Delonix regia
(Flame tree with red flowers)

Erythrina
Coral Tree

Erythrina, a large genus of approximately 120 species of semi-evergreen and deciduous perennials, is native to tropical and subtropical regions throughout the world. These spiny, spreading plants include trees, shrubs, and sub-shrubs, and are often grown as specimen plants. They feature attractive foliage consisting of alternate leaves, which are divided into three-pinnate leaflets. The terminal leaflet of each leaf is larger than the others, and sometimes differently shaped. *Erythrina* plants produce dazzling light orange to flame-red blossoms, which are protected by branches covered in sharp prickles.

The following are the most common *Erythrina* species grown in the Arabian Gulf region:

Erythrina caffra, lucky bean tree: The lucky bean tree, native to east and south Africa, is a wide-spreading, semi-evergreen tree. This plant reaches an adult height of 12–18m, and spreads to a width of 10–15m. It has prickly foliage, both branches and leaves, with each leaf divided into three broadly ovate leaflets, the longest of which can reach 9cm. The leaves may fall briefly in January and February, in preparation for the spring flowering. *Erythrina caffra* produces dense terminal racemes of long, orange-scarlet flowers. Each raceme measures 15cm in length, and each blossom is approximately 5cm long. These dramatic flowers feature broad, strongly arching standard petals.

Erythrina crista-galli, coral tree, cock's comb: Native of Argentina, Brazil, Paraguay, and Uruguay, the coral tree is a fast-growing, open-branched, deciduous species. Ranging in height from 6–10m, and spreading to a width of 3–4m, its branches have spiny, leathery, deep green leaves, and prickly stalks measuring 30cm or longer. Each stalk has three triangular leaflets, each about 10cm long, and the largest leaflet is ovate-oblong heart-shaped. This tree's other common name, cock's comb, is derived from its deep red flowers. These blossoms, each 5–6cm in length, emerge in terminal racemes, between 30–60cm long, at the end of the tree's branches.

Opposite page
Erythrina crista-galli
Cock's comb flowers

Above
Erythrina crista-galli
Cock's comb flowers and tree

Opposite page
Erythrina caffra
Lucky bean tree

Above
Erythrina caffra
Lucky bean tree flowers, trunk and fruits

Right
Erythrina variegata
Tiger's claw leaves

***Erythrina variegata*, tiger's claw:** *Erythrina variegata*, commonly known as tiger's claw, is native to the tropical regions of India and China. This tree quickly spreads from its natural distribution and has become one of the most popular of the ornamental trees. It is a spiny, deciduous, fast growing, spreading species, composed of many branches covered in prickles. These trees grow to a maximum height of between 18 and 25m, and a width ranging from 8–15m. Tiger's claw foliage is a rich, vibrant green, composed of leaves on long stalks, 25–40cm in length, each with three ovate to broadly diamond-shaped leaflets.

These leaflets can be 15–20cm long, and are often variegated light green and yellow along the main veins. This foliage serves as a backdrop for the tree's scarlet or crimson flowers, measuring 5–6cm in length, and emerging in dense, terminal racemes, up to 20cm long. The tree often loses its leaves during the dry season.

Care: *Erythrina* trees thrive when planted in fertile, moist, well-drained soil in a location that gets full sun. During the growing season trees in this genus should be watered freely, and should also receive a monthly application of a balanced liquid fertilizer. Trim *Erythrina* trees regularly to retain a pleasing shape.

Propagation: From seeds, or by rooting semi-ripe cuttings. When propagating this tree using cuttings, place large branches in soil in a large container.

Pests and diseases: Trees in the *Erythrina* genus are susceptible to red spider mite damage. These pests should be treated by a licensed exterminator.

Uses: The young leaves of *Erythrina* variegata are edible.

Above
Erythrina variegata
Tiger's claw flowers, fruits, trunk and tree

Eucalyptus
Gum Tree, Ironbark Tree

Native to Australia, *Eucalyptus* is a large, varied genus of approximately 500 species of evergreen, perennial, fast-growing timber trees and shrubs. Plants in this genus can range from 2m to over 50m tall, and from 3m to a massive 35m in width. Drought resistant, these trees are often valued for their aromatic foliage and attractive bark. When the trees are young, the leaves are opposite. As the trees mature, the leaves become alternate. The flowers of *Eucalyptus* trees have sepals and petals which are connected to form a cap, called an operculum. This cap, which fits over the stamens in the bud, is pushed off as the flower opens. The stamens which are then exposed may be white, creamy yellow or red in color. *Eucalyptus* trees produce woody capsule-like fruits, which contain seeds. The capsules, like the varied sizes of the trees in this genus, differ greatly in size and shape depending on the species.

Eucalyptus varieties grown in the Middle East are often planted as privacy screens or windbreaks. In contrast, smaller, root-bound varieties may not grow much larger in maturity than the size they are when first planted. Although all *Eucalyptus* trees are messy, with leaves falling year-round, they are a popular addition to parks and gardens worldwide, because of their interesting foliage, flowers, and seeds.

The following are the most common *Eucalyptus* species grown in the Arabian Gulf region:

Eucalyptus camaldulensis (synonym *Eucalyptus rostrata*), red gum: The red gum is a spreading, dense tree, growing to a mature height of

Opposite page
Eucalyptus camaldulensis
Red gum flowers

Above
Eucalyptus camaldulensis
Red gum flowers
and leaves

15–50m and a width of 15–35m. It has a smooth, grey or whitish blue trunk, which is sometimes streaked or tinted reddish pink. Young red gum leaves are ovate to broadly lance-shaped, and grey-green in color. Adult leaves reach a final length of up to 30cm long, are lance-shaped, and are usually mid-green or sometimes grey-green in color. In the summertime, umbels of seven to 11 blossoms, white in color, are produced. Red gum trees have deep root systems, which can harm building foundations and drainage systems. For this reason, they are typically planted in farms on along roadsides, far from houses.

***Eucalyptus gunnii*, cider gum:** Native to Australia and the island of Tasmania, cider gum trees range in height from 10–25m and spread to a width of 6–15m. These dense, erect trees have smooth, whitish-green bark that is shed annually in late summer to reveal yellowish- to greyish-green new bark. This new growth sometimes has a flushed pink or orange hue.

Young cider gum leaves are ovate to rounded, mid-green, and often glaucous. Adult leaves reach a final length of 5–8cm, are elliptic or ovate to broadly lance-shaped, and grey-green in color. In summer through to autumn, this tree produces white to cream colored blossoms in umbels of three.

Care: *Eucalyptus* trees thrive when planted in fertile, moist, well-drained soil in a location that receives full sun. During the growing season this type of tree should be watered freely, and a balanced liquid fertilizer applied monthly. Trim *Eucalyptus* trees regularly to help them retain a pleasant shape.

Propagation: From seed.

Pests and diseases: Trees in the *Eucalyptus* genus are susceptible to pests such as silver leaf, oedema, and sucker insect, all of which should be treated by a licensed exterminator.

Uses: Parts of the red gum tree are useful both industrially and medicinally. The wood of the red gum tree is used to make furniture. The leaves of this tree can be used to make paper, and also produce an oil, which is often an ingredient in soaps and perfumes. Medicinally, red gum oil, when combined in a 1:1 ratio with olive oil, can be used as a rub to ease the pain of rheumatism.

Opposite page
Eucalyptus camaldulensis
Red gum flowers, trunk and trees

Above
Eucalyptus gunnii
Cider gum leaves and tree

Ficus
Ficus Tree

Known commonly as ornamental figs, *Ficus* trees, native to Asia, have spread throughout the world. The genus *Ficus* contains about 850 species of evergreen, perennial, open-headed, fast-growing trees and shrubs. This large genus includes plants ranging in height from 2m to over 60m, and spreading from 1m to as much as 40m in diameter. While smaller species are often popular as houseplants, larger *Ficus* trees may be planted near factories, to reduce air pollution, or as natural wind barriers for houses in coastal areas. All plants in the *Ficus* genus produce figs, some of which are edible, including red and green figs. *Ficus* plants are popular with gardeners, as they are easy to propagate and are tolerant of heat, humidity, and sand in the air. However, the branches of *Ficus* plants exude a white latex substance when cut, and this sap may irritate the skin.

The following are the most common *Ficus* species grown in the Arabian Gulf region:

Ficus benghalensis, banyan, Indian fig: *Ficus benghalensis*, commonly known as the banyan tree, is native to India and neighboring countries. Its name is derived from the Hindu word *banian*, meaning *trader*. Banyans are evergreens, with many spreading, often horizontal branches supported by multiple prop roots. One banyan tree may have thousands of trunks, spreading to a width of 150–200m. The largest banyan tree on record is on the island of Sri Lanka. It has 350 large trunks and over 3,000 small ones. Although they may have a massive girth, banyan trees reach a mature height of only 20–30m. Their foliage consists of elliptic to broadly ovate, leathery, deep green leaves, each 13–25cm long. These leaves have a flushed bronze hue when the tree is young, developing a distinct pattern of pale veins as the plant matures. The tree produces round, red figs, about 2cm in diameter. These fruits grow in pairs; they are not, however, good to eat.

Opposite page
Ficus benghalensis
Banyan tree

Above
Ficus benghalensis
Banyan tree fruits

Banyan trees have a wide, spreading root system which can destroy streets, building foundations, drainage systems, and even interfere with electricity lines. For this reason, the tree is usually planted outside of the city, on farms. In the Middle East, banyans can be placed in desert regions, where the roots hold the sand and prevent soil erosion.

Ficus benjamina (synonym *Ficus nitida*), weeping Chinese banyan: Native to India, the weeping Chinese banyan is an attractive, bushy tropical plant. This evergreen tree has spreading, often horizontal branches supported by prop roots, and features leathery, glossy, dark green leaves which are a lighter hue on their underside. One cultivar of this plant, *Ficus benjamina* Variegata has white-splashed leaves. Each elliptic to broadly ovate leaf is 5–13cm long, tapering to a slender, twisted point. These trees produce pairs of spherical to oblong figs, measuring about 1cm in length. Figs are green when they first emerge, ripening to pink or orange-red and finally maturing to black. Often sold as an indoor plant, *Ficus benjamina* can also be a successful addition to the outside garden, where it can reach heights of up to 30m and spread to a width of 15m.

Ficus deltoidea, mistletoe fig: Native to Borneo and the Philippines, the mistletoe fig is an evergreen shrub or small tree, reaching a mature height of only 5–7m, and spreading to a width of 1–3m. This tree, usually bushy when cultivated domestically but sometimes epiphytic in the wild, has broadly spoon-shaped to obovate, leathery leaves, measuring 4–8cm in length. This foliage is bright green on the top side and rust-red to olive brown beneath. These trees produce pairs of spherical to ellipsoid figs, measuring about 1cm in diameter. Figs are dull yellow when they first emerge, ripening to orange and finally maturing to red. The mistletoe fig is commonly an indoor plant, especially in hot climates, although it can be successfully grown as an outdoor plant if placed in a shaded area of the garden.

Ficus elastica, India rubber fig: The India rubber fig is a large, many-branched, wide-spreading, evergreen tree. This *Ficus* species, similar to the banyan, ranges 30–60m in height

Opposite page
Ficus benjamina
Weeping Chinese banyan tree

Above left
Ficus benjamina
Weeping Chinese banyan tree leaves

Above right
Ficus benjamina Variegata
Weeping Chinese banyan tree leaves

and spreads to a width of 20–60m. The bark of this tree is silver-grey, and its foliage consists of smooth, oblong to elliptic, leathery, glossy, dark green leaves, often red-flushed with prominent ivory to reddish veins. Each leaf can grow to a length of 30–45cm. The India rubber fig has a unique pattern for new foliage growth. The leaves develop inside a red sheath, which grows larger as the new leaf develops. When it is mature, the leaf opens and the sheath drops off the plant. Inside each new leaf is another immature leaf, waiting to develop. The India rubber fig makes a striking addition to any large garden or park.

Ficus elastica 'Decora' has broadly elliptic leaves which are flushed-red on the underside. The leaves develop creamy white midribs as the plant matures.

Ficus elastica 'Doescheri' features unusual foliage consisting of leaves which are mottled grey-green, creamy yellow, and white, with pink stalks and midribs. This plant produces clusters of yellow-orange to red, berry-like figs.

Ficus lyrata, banjo fig, fiddle-leaf fig: Native to the tropical regions of West Africa, the banjo fig is an open, evergreen tree. Reaching a mature height of 20–30m, and a width of 10m, this tree gets it common names, banjo and fiddle-leaf fig, from its leaves, which are shaped like the musical instrument. Each leathery, glossy, dark green leaf can grow to a length of 25–45cm, and has an irregularly corrugated pattern on its top side. *Ficus lyrata* produces spherical figs, singly or in pairs, each about 3cm in diameter. This fruit ripens to a green hue with white dots, and only emerges on mature trees planted in open locations. The banjo fig is commonly an indoor plant, especially in hot climates, but can be successfully grown as an outdoor plant if placed in a shaded area of the garden.

***Ficus macrophylla*, Australian banyan:** Native to Australia, hence its common name, the Australian banyan is a large, wide-spreading evergreen, perfect for large gardens or parks. This banyan-like tree has aerial roots, some of which may become props. *Ficus macrophylla* commonly grows to a height of approximately 10m, although in its native habitat it can reach a mature height of up to 55m and spread to a

Above
Ficus sp.
Ficus tree and leaves

Left
Ficus elastica
India rubber fig
tree and leaves

Above left
Ficus macrophylla
Australian banyan tree and fruit

Above right
Ficus lyrata
Banjo fig tree and leaves

width of 20–40m. This tree has leathery, mid-green, hairless leaves, oblong to elliptic or ovate in shape, averaging 25cm in length. Its leaves are usually a paler shade on the underside, and have rust-red scales. The Australian banyan bears clusters of yellow-green, berry-like figs.

***Ficus religiosa*, Peepal tree (Arabic: *lesan al asfour*):** The Peepal tree is a large, semi-deciduous tree, averaging 20m tall and wide, making it appropriate for both public and private landscaping. Native to India, this species of *Ficus* has brown bark and large, shiny heart-shaped leaves which can grow up to 20cm in length. While mature foliage is green, new leaves are pinkish-copper in color. *Ficus religiosa* has erratic growth patterns, and requires regular pruning.

***Ficus retusa,* Indian laurel:** The Indian laurel is a dense evergreen with smooth tannish-grey bark and leathery, deep green, pointed oval leaves, averaging 10cm in length. The fruit of this tree is grey-green, berry-like figs. Due to its adaptability, moderate height (13m), and dense growth, the Indian laurel is widely used as landscaping for roadsides. This tree can be pruned into globe or cube shapes, and may also be planted to form natural privacy screens.

Care: Members of the *Ficus* genus thrive when planted in fertile, moist, well-drained

soil in a location where they are exposed to full sun. During the growing season these trees should be watered freely, and should also receive a monthly application of a high-nitrogen fertilizer. Trim *Ficus* trees regularly to encourage balanced growth.

Propagation: From cuttings or by layering. *Ficus* trees can also be propagated from seed, which commonly happens in the wild. Birds drop banyan tree seeds into the top branches of palms and other trees. These seeds then sprout in the treetops, and branches develop. The branches send down roots to the ground, and these roots support the branches. The root supports grow into trunks, and develop more new branches. As the banyan develops and matures, the host tree is strangled and dies.

Pests and diseases: Members of the genus *Ficus* are susceptible to red spider mite, thrip, mealy bug, and scale insect damage. All of these pest should be treated by a licensed exterminator.

Uses: Several trees in the *Ficus* genus produce materials which are industrially useful. The wood of the Indian fig tree is soft and porous. It also produces a white, sticky latex substance, which is an ingredient in birdlime. Birdlime is used by hunters to capture birds. *Ficus elastica* produces a similar milky latex substance, which is a source of rubber.

Above
Ficus religiosa
Peepal tree,
leaves and fruits

Above
Ficus microcarpa
Chinese banyan

Above
Ficus Binnendijkii
Long-leaf fig fruits, leaves and tree

Gliricidia sepium
Mexican Lilac

Native to Central America, Mexico, and Ecuador, *Gliricidia* is a genus of only five distinct species of perennial, deciduous, evergreen plants. Classified as large shrubs or small flowering trees, plants in this genus range from 6–15m in height.

***Gliricidia sepium*, Mexican lilac:** A fast-growing evergreen, *Gliricidia sepium* is a small to medium-sized, thornless, leguminous tree. Commonly known as the Mexican lilac, this plant grows to an average height of 10–12m, although particularly hardy specimens can reach up to 20m when fully mature. It may have a single trunk or multiple trunks, each measuring an average of 50–70mm in diameter, with some trunks growing to a girth of as much as 1m. The trunk is covered in smooth bark, which can range from whitish grey to a deep red-brown in color. The trunk, as well as the tree's branches, are often flecked with small white lenticels. Mexican lilacs have an open, rounded crown and foliage consisting of opposite, pinnate, bright green leaves. Each leaf, measuring about 30cm in length, is divided into seven to 15 opposite, elliptic leaflets. Each leaflet is 2–7cm long and 1–3cm wide, with a pointed tip and rounded base.

Leafless when in flower, *Gliricidia sepium* produces dense clusters of colorful whitish-pink or purple blossoms. Each raceme, emerging from the plant's leaf axils, is 5–15cm long and bears 20–40 blooms. Each tiny bell-shaped flower has a green, glabrous calyx, pea-shaped corolla, and five strongly unequal petals. The standard petal is round and nearly erect, approximately 20mm long, with a pale yellow spot at the flower's base. The keel petals are smaller, 15–20mm long and 4–7mm wide.

In April and May, *Gliricidia sepium* produce fruit in the form of pods, measuring 10–15cm long and 2cm wide. These fruits are initially green, ripening to a yellow-brown, almost woody pod when mature. Fruits typically ripen in 45–60 days, depending on the climate, and each pod contains between four and 10 nearly round, brown seeds.

Mexican lilacs are a beautiful addition to gardens, attracting bees, butterflies, and birds, and as such are popular choices for landscaping.

Caution: ***Gliricidia sepium*** **roots, bark and seeds are poisonous if ingested.**

Opposite page
Gliricidia sepium
Mexican lilac flowers

Above
Gliricidia sepium
Mexican lilac
leaves and fruits

Care: Mexican lilacs thrive in sunny locations, so it is important to regularly prune any surrounding hedges to control shading. Place trees in well-drained soil, water daily, and mist plants to raise humidity.

Propagation: From cutting or seed. To propagate using seeds, soak the seeds in hot water, allow them to cool off during the night, and sow seeds the next morning in individual containers. Once the seeds have sprouted, transplant seedlings while the ground is still moist. Place seedlings in a partially shaded location, spacing plants 1–2m apart.

Pests and diseases: *Gliricidia sepium* is susceptible to aphid, mealy bug, and scale insect damage. All of these pests must be treated by a licensed exterminator.

Uses: Mexican lilac is used in many tropical and sub-tropical countries for a variety of agricultural purposes. It is sometimes planted in rows to separate crops, acting as a living fence and a natural windbreak. The trees may be interspersed with other plants to provide shade for crops such as coffee, vanilla, tea, and cacao. In Sri Lanka, Mexican lilac has been grown between rows of coconuts and found to be an excellent organic fertilizer. The foliage of the Mexican lilac is rich is nitrogen; the leaves are often used as green manure, and the tree can be made into mulch. In Africa, Mexican lilac is planted with native crops to serve as an alternative to expensive chemical fertilizers, as it naturally fixes nitrogen into the soil, significantly boosting crop yields. Mexican lilac blooms also attract honey bees.

Wood from the *Gliricidia sepium* tree is highly resistant to termites and decay, and as such is used for a variety of purposes. Industrially, the wood is used to make building poles, charcoal, containers, crates, and pallets, as well as posts for heavy construction. Its smooth finish makes it a popular choice for woodworking, and it is sometimes used to create furniture and tool handles. Mexican lilac timbers also make good firewood, as it burns slowly and produces little smoke.

In addition to its wood, the foliage of the Mexican lilac is also useful. Its leaves have a high nutritional value, consisting of up to 20–30% crude protein, and 15% crude fiber. They are used as a high protein supplement to low quality cattle feeds such as grass, straw, and other crop residues.

Several parts of the *Gliricidia sepium* tree are useful for pest control. The toxic properties of the seeds and bark make them useful as a rat poison. The leaves, when crushed, produce a fetid smell, and can be rubbed on dogs and cattle to rid them of fleas and ticks. Fresh leaves can even be used by people, rubbed on the skin to act as a natural insect repellent.

Medicinally, various parts of the Mexican lilac tree can be used internally and externally, to treat a wide variety of ailments. In Guatemala, the bark and leaves of the Mexican lilac are used to treat human skin diseases. The sap from the bark, leaves and roots have been used for wound healing, and in the treatment of scabies. In Panama, a salve made from boiling the leaves of this tree is used to treat many skin ailments, including urticaria, rash, burns, and erysipelas. In the Philippines, a leaf extract is used to remove external parasites. Internally, medicines derived from this plant are used for headache, bruises, colds, cough, fever, fatigue, gangrene, and gonorrhea.

Opposite page
Gliricidia sepium
Mexican lilac

Handroanthus chrysanthus
Golden Trumpet Tree

Handroanthus is a genus of 30 species of tender perennial, flowering trees. Ranging in height from 9m to over 35m, these deciduous plants are native to Central and South America.

Handroanthus chrysanthus **(synonym *Tabebuia chrysantha*), golden trumpet tree:** The golden trumpet tree is a rounded to spreading deciduous tree, reaching a maximum height of 25m and a width of 18m. These trees feature foliage consisting of opposite, palmate leaves, each leaf composed of five lance-shaped to obovate, entire or toothed leaflets which are mid-green in color. The leaves have a light dusting of star-shaped hairs on their upper surfaces, with a more dense covering of hair underneath. The central leaflets can grow up to 18cm long. Plants in this species are named for their golden yellow, trumpet-shaped flowers. These sweetly scented blossoms grow to 5cm in length, and are borne in panicles in the springtime.

Caution: While these trees make an attractive addition to any garden, care should be taken, as parts of plant are poisonous if ingested.

Care: Golden trumpet trees flourish in tropical conditions of sun and high humidity. These plants require daily watering and misting; water freely in summer, and moderately in winter. *Handroanthus chrysanthus* should be placed in well-drained soil, and this soil should be enriched monthly with a compound fertilizer during the growing season.

Propagation: By seed, air layering, or by rooting semi-ripe stem cuttings. When propagating by seed, harvest seeds as soon as the pods crack open. Fresh seeds will germinate within one or two weeks after planting.

Pests and diseases: These trees are susceptible to red spider mite damage. These pests should be treated by a licensed exterminator.

Opposite page and above
Handroanthus chrysanthus
Golden trumpet tree flowers

Hibiscus tiliaceus
Sea Hibiscus, Cottonwood

Native to tropical and subtropical regions throughout the world, *Hibiscus* is a genus of more than 200 species of shrubs, trees, and herbaceous perennials. These deciduous and evergreen plants range from 1–10m in height, and spread from 1–8m wide, depending on the species. It belongs to a family that is unmistakable when in flower, the cotton or hibiscus family.

***Hibiscus tiliaceus*, sea hibiscus, cottonwood:** Native to Old World tropical regions extending to Australia, *Hibiscus tiliaceus* is one of the few *Hibiscus* species successfully grown in the Arabian Gulf. Attractive, fast growing, evergreen, flowering shrubs or small trees, sea hibiscus grow to a height of 4–20m, with a short, crooked trunk measuring up to 15cm in diameter. This smooth trunk, covered in grey or light brown bark, supports a broad crown of wide, low spreading branches. The branches are crooked, long and flexible. Young branches, buds and flowers are densely covered with short soft hairs, and the branches curve as the tree matures. Twigs are stout, with rings at their nodes, and they grow darker brown in hue and become hairless over time. From these branches emerge foliage consisting of alternate, simple, large, heart-shaped leaves with downy undersides and entire or toothed edges. Leaves grow on leafstalks measuring 5–13cm in length, are usually leathery in texture, and are shiny and dark green in color. Some varieties feature variegated or purplish foliage.

During the flowering season, which begins in April, this tree produces axillary clusters of bright yellow flowers, funnel-shaped with five petals, a dark, reddish-brown center, and a dark red stigma. Blossoms are about 10–15cm in diameter when fully open, and grow in clusters at or near the ends of twigs. Hibiscus flowers are short lived, opening in the morning, after sunrise, and turning orangey-brown before falling on the same evening or the following day. Sea hibiscus produce fruit in the form of small, woody spheres or capsules, densely covered with small whitish grey star-shaped hairs, which open into five segments, releasing three to five tiny, kidney-shaped seeds.

Care: Hibiscus trees thrive in sunny locations, can stand brackish water, and are tolerant of salt spray. This makes them an excellent choice for gardens in coastal areas. They are particularly suited to sandy and moist soils, although they can grow well under drier conditions and in a variety of soils. Soil should be enriched monthly with a balanced liquid fertilizer during the growing season. Sea hibiscus require daily watering, particularly during the summer months, and also need misting in order to maintain humidity. Regular pruning and sucker removal are necessary for the trees to keep a balanced, attractive shape.

Opposite page
Hibiscus tiliaceus
Sea hibiscus flowers

Above
Hibiscus tiliaceus
Sea hibiscus

Propagation: Hibiscus trees can be propagated in spring by air layering, or by inserting semi-ripe cuttings with bottom heat. Cuttings should be between 20 and 40cm long and 0.5–1cm thick, and root well when rooting hormone is used. Alternatively, these plants can be grown from seeds. To prepare seeds, file the back of the seed with an emery board or sand paper, and soak for at least 24 hours prior to planting. Take care not to reach the tender embryo inside the seed when filing. After soaking, the seed can be planted in sandy, moist soil. Seedlings, which will usually emerge in a week or two, should be placed in a well-lighted area. They can grow 60–80cm in the first year, if planted in good soil and watered regularly.

Pests and diseases: Sea hibiscus trees are susceptible to a wide range of pests, including aphid, whitefly, mealy bug, powdery mildew, red spider mite, and scale insect. These should all be treated by a licensed exterminator.

Uses: All parts of the *Hibiscus tiliaceus* tree are useful. The bark of the tree contains tough fibers used for making rope and to caulk ships. The wood is used in sea craft construction, as firewood, and for wood carvings, as well as for making high-quality furniture. The stems and branches

are long and flexible, and are used as living fence posts. Young leaves and roots can be cooked and eaten as vegetables, and in Southeast Asia mature leaves are used as feed for livestock.

Medicinally, the leaves, bark, and roots of this tree are used to cool fevers, soothe coughs and remove phlegm from the chest. In traditional medicine in Southeast Asia, fresh bark is soaked in water and used to treat dysentery. The flower buds of this plant can be chewed to relieve a dry throat. In Guam, crushed sea hibiscus flowers are applied to abscesses, and in other areas fresh flowers boiled in milk are used to treat ear infections. The Polynesians use the slimy sap of the bark, branches and flower buds as a mild laxative or lubricant for mothers during childbirth.

For landscaping purposes, sea hibiscus are popular as ornamental and shade trees, and can often be seen in resort landscapes where they serve as a natural windbreak for strong sea winds. They are also widely used in Asian countries as a subject for the art of bonsai. Sea Hibiscus trees can be kept in containers if properly pruned and re-potted as necessary. When planting in the garden, consideration should be given as to location; this tree should only be planted where there is no possibility of damage to structures such as pavements or pools.

Above
Hibiscus tiliaceus
Sea hibiscus flower during the day (yellow), in the evening (orangey-brown), leaves and fruits

Jacaranda mimosifolia
Blue Jacaranda

The genus *Jacaranda*, comprised of about 49 different species of deciduous or evergreen trees, is indigenous to tropical and subtropical regions of South America, including Bolivia, Brazil and Argentina.

***Jacaranda mimosifolia*, blue jacaranda:** Reaching a height of 10–20m and a spread of 7–10m, the blue jacaranda is a fast growing, attractive, flowering tree with a round-headed crown of delicate foliage. At its center is a short, stout trunk, often well-branched and covered in grey-brown bark. The bark is smooth when the tree is young, though it eventually becomes finely scaly. Spreading out from the trunk are low branches, slender and slightly bent, light reddish-brown in color. The branches support foliage consisting of elegant, fern-like, opposite, broad, bi-pinnately compound leaves. Each leaf, measuring 25–45cm long, is composed of between 13–25 pairs of small, narrowly elliptic, softly hairy, bright to mid-green leaflets. Deciduous to semi-deciduous, the leaves often fall in April, but are immediately replaced with new ones. The tree loses its lower leaves with age.

Blue jacarandas are named and known for their beautiful, long-lasting blue flowers. Blooming in continuous cycles for as long as two months, from spring through early summer, the tree produces terminal, broadly pyramidal, large, airy panicles of blossoms. Each panicle, measuring 20–30cm long, is composed of large numbers of tubular, narrowly bell-shaped blooms that are tightly packed together. Panicles are borne on leafless branches or those with young foliage. The showy, fragrant flowers, 3.5–5cm long, are made up of five unequal petals joining as a long

Opposite page
Jacaranda mimosifolia
Blue jacaranda flowers

Above
Jacaranda mimosifolia
Blue jacaranda
fruits and leaves

corolla tube, mounted on a red-brown stalk. Blossoms are white-throated, and petals are glowing purple-blue or white in hue.

At the end of the flowering season, the tree's vibrant blossoms are followed by one or two flattened, rounded, fleshy, disc-like, pods. The pods, measuring 5–7cm across, are green or dark brown, becoming woody as they ripen. They split open along the edges, expelling large numbers of flat, very dark brown-winged seeds.

Care: *Jacaranda* trees can be grown in a range of climates, including the harsh Arabian Gulf. The trees thrive in tropical and warm, temperate climates. They also grow in cooler regions, even in places where light frost occurs. However, in these areas the trees are smaller, slower-growing, and do not flower as well.

Blue jacarandas do best when placed in locations receiving full sun, and planted in well-drained, sandy soil. Enrich soil monthly with a balanced liquid, high-potassium fertilizer, and mulch around the roots, over moist soil, with organic material such as compost, straw, or bark. The layer of mulch should be no thicker than 50mm.

Jacaranda trees require regular pruning. Trim smaller branches in early spring, and keep excess branches cut, to prevent the weight of the tree from splitting the trunk. It is recommended to keep one main trunk, with some major branches leading off from the middle. Remove suckers that grow vertically. Regular pruning will allow the tree to maintain a balanced shape, and showcase the tree's flowers.

Water *Jacaranda* trees freely during the growing season; mulch will help to retain soil moisture in summer.

Propagation: By seed or from cuttings. To propagate by seed, prepare fresh seeds by soaking them in water for 24 hours; germination should occur within 10–12 days. To grow from branch cuttings, root semi-ripe cuttings with bottom heat in summer.

Pests and diseases: Plants in the *Jacaranda* genus are susceptible to whitefly, termite and red spider mite damage. These pests should be treated by a licensed exterminator.

Uses: Many parts of the *Jacaranda* tree are used for a variety of purposes. Jacaranda blooms attract bees for honey. The wood is used for turnery and bowl carving, and is also a source of firewood. The tree's seed-pods are commonly used to decorate Christmas trees and in dried floral arrangements. Medicinally, jacaranda leaves are a vulnerary, and the bark and roots are used in the treatment of syphilis.

For landscaping purposes, *Jacaranda* trees are grown as ornamental plants in many parts of the world. They are popular as specimen trees, and make an excellent shade or street tree, lawn tree, or park tree. They are used in commercial landscapes, and in public open spaces. They can also be cultivated as a bonsai specimen. Care should be taken when choosing where to place trees in the garden, as the blooms continuously fall and carpet the ground. For this reason, these trees should not be planted near pools.

Opposite page
Jacaranda mimosifolia
Blue jacaranda

Kigelia africana
Sausage Tree

Native of tropical Africa, *Kigelia* is a genus of only one species of perennial, evergreen or semi-deciduous tree. This flowering, fast-growing, medium-sized tree grows to heights ranging from 6–25m.

Kigelia africana (synonym *Kigelia pinnata*), sausage tree: Reaching maturity within four to five years after germination, depending on the climate, *Kigelia africana* is a freely branching tree with robust stems. Its sturdy trunk, covered in light brown to grey bark, supports a dense rounded to spreading crown, measuring 5–20m in width. The trunk is smooth when the tree is young, eventually peeling as the tree ages.

The sausage tree features foliage consisting of large, pinnate leaves, borne in opposite pairs, crowded near the ends of its branches. Each leaf is 30–50cm long, and composed of nine to 11 oblong to obovate leaflets, plus a terminal leaflet. Each small leaflet is 6–10cm long, leathery, slightly glossy, and mid- to deep green in color.

Blooming from late summer through autumn, *Kigelia africana* produces pendent panicles of fragrant, bell-shaped flowers. Each panicle, 1–2m long, is composed of six to 12 blossoms. Flowers are yellowish-green in bud, opening to rich brownish red at night. Measuring 10–15cm across, the flowers open one at a time and attract birds and insects, which serve to pollinate the plant.

Kigelia africana takes its common name, sausage tree, from its large, cylindrically shaped fruit. These woody pods measure 30–100cm in length, 18cm in width, and weigh as much as 5–10kg. The fruits remain on the thickened, flowering stems for several months. This hefty fruit is grey-brown when ripe, with fibrous pulp and numerous seeds.

Caution: Although sausage tree seeds are eaten by wild animals, they are poisonous if ingested by people.

Opposite page
Kigelia africana
Sausage tree flowers

Above
Kigelia africana
Sausage tree buds and fruits at various stages of growth

Right
Kigelia africana
Sausage tree

Care: *Kigelia africana* trees flourish in dry locations where they can receive full sun all day. They require little special care, aside from moderately fertile, well-drained soil, and monthly applications of a balanced liquid fertilizer. Regular pruning after flowering will help the tree maintain a balanced shape.

Propagation: From seed or cuttings. Propagate by seed in springtime; prepare seeds by soaking them in boiling water for one minute, to aid germination. If using cuttings, sticks cut from the tree and planted directly into the soil will root readily.

Pests and diseases: Sausage trees are susceptible to whitefly, mealy bug, and red spider mite damage. These pests should be treated by a licensed exterminator.

Uses: *Kigelia africana* is a popular shade and street tree in tropical Africa and Australia. It is commonly planted alongside dams on farms and game reserves. In its native Africa, the tree is a food source for foraging hippos, baboons, and giraffes. The durable wood this tree produces is used to make shelving and fruit boxes, and in Botswana and Zimbabwe the trunks are used in making dugout canoes. The roots of *Kigelia africana* yield a bright yellow dye.

Various parts of the sausage tree are refined for cosmetic and medical purposes. Steroid chemicals found in the tree are currently added to commercially available shampoos and facial creams. Medicinally, traditional remedies prepared from crushed, dried or fresh fruits have been used for topical skin treatments. Poultices of this fruit are known to relieve various skin afflictions ranging from fungal infections, boils, psoriasis, and eczema, to more serious diseases such as leprosy and skin cancer. Internally, derivatives of this plant have been used to treat ulcers, sores, syphilis, dysentery, ringworm, tapeworm, malaria, diabetes, and even the common toothache.

For landscaping purposes, *Kigelia africana* is suitable for planting in large gardens and municipal parks as an ornamental or shade tree, and can even be groomed successfully for bonsai. Locations for this tree should be chosen carefully, however, as the falling fruit can cause serious injury to people and damage vehicles parked under the trees. Additionally, this tree has an aggressively invasive root system, and so should be planted clear of buildings, paving, and pools.

Above
Kigelia africana
Sausage tree
trunk and leaves

Lagerstroemia
Crepe Myrtle, Pride of India

A native of tropical regions from Asia to Australia, *Lagerstroemia* is a genus of more than 50 species of perennial, deciduous and evergreen shrubs and trees. Ranging in height from 1–24m, and spreading 2–10m wide, these trees are cultivated for their conical, brightly colored panicles of flowers, with characteristic crinkled petals, and their often peeling bark. Although the foliage of the trees varies greatly by species, their leaves are usually oppositely arranged. *Lagerstroemia* are grown as specimen plants, and may also be planted as a group to compose screens or hedges.

The following are the most common *Lagerstroemia* species grown in the Arabian Gulf region:

Lagerstroemia indica, **crepe flower, crepe myrtle:** An upright, deciduous or semi-evergreen plant, the crepe myrtle is a slow-growing small tree or large shrub. Native to both India and China, this tree ranges in height from 1–12m and spreads up to 6m wide. The trunks of this multi-trunked, low-branched tree are smooth and peeling, shedding pinkish-grey and brown bark, flaking off to reveal an attractive pink inner bark.

Crepe myrtle feature foliage composed of opposite, simple, small, smooth-edged, obovate to oblong, dark glossy green leaves. Each leaf is 3–8cm long, bronze when young and changing to yellow, orange, and red in autumn. This foliage serves as a backdrop for the tree's dramatic clusters of very showy white, pink, red, or purple flowers. These blossoms, emerging in panicles 9–20cm long, measure only 2–2.5cm across. The tree blooms from late summer to autumn, and flowers for a period of 60–120 days. *Lagerstroemia indica* gets its common name, crepe flower, from the blossoms' crinkly petals that resemble the material crepe.

After flowering, *Lagerstroemia indica* produce oval or round, small, brown or black fruits. These fruits mature and split to release disk-shaped seeds.

Lagerstroemia speciosa, **Pride of India:** This spreading, freely branching, evergreen tree reaches a mature height of 10–45m, and spreads to a width of 5–10m. *Lagerstroemia speciosa* has a fissured trunk covered with peeling, light brown to light grey bark. The trunk averages 100–150cm in diameter, and supports branches from which emerge foliage consisting of opposite, simple, ovate to elliptic-oblong leaves. Each leaf is 8–20cm long, 3–7cm wide, and has an acute apex, with a very short stalk (petiole). The young foliage is bronzy-red, and older leaves are grey-green above and sepia-flushed beneath. As leaves mature they develop a leathery texture.

Commonly known as the Pride of India, from spring to autumn this tree produces erect, open panicles of pale to deep lavender blossoms. Each panicle is 20–40cm long, and each flower is made up of six or more ruffled petals. Some varieties of this plant flower in white or dark pink lilac-like hues. These flowers make a striking display, particularly in clusters.

The Pride of India loses its leaves in winter; before dropping they turn an attractive, orangey-pink color. New leaves appear in March, and a second flowering is possible in early autumn.

After flowering, *Lagerstroemia speciosa* produce globose fruits, green to olive-green when new and ripening from brown to an almost black, woody texture. Each

Opposite page
Lagerstroemia indica
Crepe myrtle flowers

Above
Lagerstroemia indica
Crepe myrtle

capsule-like fruit is 2cm long with a spike at the tip. Once mature the fruits split open along five or six sutures to expose neatly packed seeds inside.

The Pride of India makes an excellent tree for patios and small gardens, and will attract bees, butterflies, and birds to any yard. It is also sometimes used in city landscaping as a roadside tree.

Care: *Lagerstroemia* trees are a viable choice for Gulf gardens, as they thrive outdoors in full sun and are tolerant of dry conditions. They do, however, require frequent fertilization with a balanced liquid fertilizer; apply every six to eight weeks. Plant in moderately fertile, well-drained soil. To truly flourish, trees in the *Lagerstroemia* genus need a soil that has been enriched with iron chelate or iron sulphate.

Care should be taken when choosing a location for *Lagerstroemia* in the garden. The leaves can be burnt by summer winds, so a sheltered position is best. This plant will grow into a small tree, and it requires regular pruning to preserve an attractive shape and develop a strong structure. Pruning should be done in late winter or early spring.

Propagation: From seed in spring. These trees can also be propagated by rooting softwood cuttings in late spring, or using semi-ripe cuttings in summer.

Pests and diseases: Trees in the *Lagerstroemia* genus are susceptible to whitefly, mealy bug, and red spider mite. These pests should be treated by a licensed exterminator. Mildew can also be a serious problem for this plant in areas with a very humid climate.

Uses: Many parts of the *Lagerstroemia speciosa* tree have medicinal uses. Herbal tea made from the dried leaves of this tree is beneficial for diabetics. This drink can also help detoxify the body and protect the liver. The bark and leaves are a natural purgative, and the roots are a stimulant and can be used to reduce fever. The fruit of this tree is used as a local application for mouth sores, and the seeds of *Lagerstroemia speciosa* are a narcotic.

Aside from its medicinal properties, the Pride of India is often planted in areas suffering from erosion. Its dense, wide-spreading root system help to fix the soil.

Above
Lagerstroemia indica
Crepe myrtle flowers and bud

Right
Lagerstroemia speciosa
Pride of India

Above

Lagerstroemia speciosa
Pride of India flowers, buds and trunk

Lawsonia inermis
Henna Tree, Mignonette Tree

Lawsonia is a genus of only one species of evergreen, flowering shrub or small tree. Native to south and west Asia, Iran, and throughout Arabia to North Africa, this large shrub or small tree reaches a mature height of 3–6m, and spreads to a width of 2–4m. Its diminutive size makes it perfect for hedges and shrub borders.

***Lawsonia inermis*, henna tree, mignonette tree:** *Lawsonia inermis* is a multi-branched tree, with spine-tipped branchlets. Its foliage consists of opposite, simple, entire, elliptic and lanceolate leaves. These leaves are mid-green in color, often with a reddish brown tinge, and are smooth, 2–5cm long, and taper to a point. They serve as a backdrop for the trees' large, dramatic clusters of flowers. The dense, pyramidal, terminal panicles, each 20–40cm long, are composed of small, fragrant blossoms. Each tiny flower has four sepals, four crumpled, broadly ovate or spoon-shaped, white to pale yellow, pink, or cinnabar-red petals, and pairs of stamens, which are found on the rim of the calyx tube. The minute ovary of this blossom is four-celled, 5mm long, and erect. Henna trees bloom in summer.

Lawsonia inermis produces small, brownish, capsule-shaped fruits. As the fruits ripen, they open irregularly into four splits. Each fruit contains between 32 and 49 charcoal colored, triangular seeds.

Care: Henna trees are perfect for gardens in the Arabian Gulf region, as they thrive outdoors in full sun and can tolerate dry conditions. They require moderately fertile, well-drained soil, as well as regular pruning to maintain a balanced shape. For best results, trim hedges in early summer.

Propagation: By seed. Henna trees can also be propagated by rooting softwood cuttings in spring or hardwood cuttings in autumn.

Pests and diseases: *Lawsonia inermis* is susceptible to red spider mite and whitefly damage. Both these pests should be treated by a licensed exterminator.

Uses: Although the blossoms of the henna plant are used to make a fragrant oil, *Lawsonia inermis* is probably most famous for the dye made from its leaves, which also gives the plant its colloquial name. Henna is commonly produced as a powder, made by drying, milling, and sifting the leaves. This powder can be mixed with lemon juice, strong tea, or other mildly acidic liquids to form a toothpaste-consistency substance. The henna mix must rest for six to 24 hours before use, to release the lawsone molecules from the leaf matter, giving it its orange-red hue.

Opposite page
Lawsonia inermis
Henna tree flowers

Above
Lawsonia inermis
Henna tree

Henna is used to make temporary tattoos and other finely detailed body art. Women throughout Asia use henna to color their finger and toe nails, fingertips, and parts of their feet. Culturally, henna is used by women to signify celebrations, such as holidays and weddings. Religiously, in Islam there are narrations by the Prophet Muhammad (peace be upon him) encouraging Muslim women to dye their nails with henna to highlight their femininity and distinguish their hands from those of men.

Henna paste can be applied using a cone, syringe, jac bottle or the fingers. The longer the paste is left on the skin, the stronger the stain will be; for best results, henna should be left for several hours. To prevent the paste from drying and flaking off the skin, it is usually sealed by dabbing a sugar and lemon mixture on top of the design. After the dye is set, the paste is brushed or scraped away. Essential oils such as tea tree, eucalyptus, cajeput, or lavender can then be rubbed over the design to improve the stain. Although the color will initially be light, it will darken over the following three days to a reddish brown. Henna applied to the palms of the hands and the soles of the feet will stain darkest and last longest, because these areas have thicker skin that absorbs more lawsone from the dye. After the stain reaches its darkest color it will gradually fade, as the stained skin cells exfoliate.

In addition to body art, henna has long been used as a hair dye. In Islam, the Prophet Muhammad (peace be upon him) used henna to dye his beard, and this tradition is still followed by Muslim men around the world today. Henna dye is also used to color wool, silk, animal skins, and animal fur such as the manes and hoofs, paws, and tails of horses, donkeys, and salukis.

Medicinally, henna paste can be used to treat a variety of ailments, both internal and external. Henna paste is great for the hair; it prevents hair loss, split ends, and dandruff. It is good for the skin, and can be used as a salve to treat eczema, scabies, and athlete's foot, as well as open wounds. Henna will strengthen brittle and cracked fingernails, and can be made into a poultice and applied to the forehead to treat headaches. Chewing henna leaves can relive pain from mouth ulcers, and tea made from boiled leaves can be used as a gargle to treat throat inflammation.

Above
Lawsonia inermis
Henna tree fruits and leaves

Leucaena leucocephala
White Leadtree

Leucaena, a small genus of 22 species of evergreens, is native to Central America from Mexico south to Peru. These trees and shrubs reach a mature height of between 7 and 15m.

***Leucaena leucocephala*, white leadtree:** The white leadtree is fast-growing, and quickly reaches its mature height of 10m. It is a perfect-sized shade tree for gardens or courtyards. *Leucaena leucocephala* has lightly textured bark, greyish-brown in color, which supports branches containing opposite, bi-pinnate leaves, about 25cm in length. Each leaf is composed of six to eight pairs of leaflets, and each leaflet has 12–16 pairs of fine, oblong or oval-shaped, mid- to bright green smaller leaflets. These tiny leaflets are 1cm long and 3mm wide. The leaves and leaflets of the white leadtree close when the weather is humid or cold, or when it is dark.

Leucaena leucocephala bears lovely, fragrant spring blossoms in the form of small white or creamy yellow fluff balls, emerging in clusters at the ends of its branches. Following the flowers are flat fruit pods, growing 10–16cm long and about 1–1.5cm wide. These pods, initially green in color and maturing to brown, have raised edges and contain 10–25 oval-shaped, brown seeds. The white leadtree is appealing to native wildlife. Its flowers attract bees looking for nectar, and its high-protein seeds attract birds and rodents. These animals help to propagate the tree though seed dispersal.

Care: The white leadtree is a good addition to Gulf gardens because it is draught tolerant. However, it needs regular pruning to maintain a pleasing shape, and fertilization every two weeks when it is young. It is also a messy tree, shedding its leaves year-round.

Propagation: *Leucaena leucocephala* can be propagated using semi-ripe root cuttings with bottom heat in summer, or by planting seeds. To propagate from seed, soak new seeds 24 hours before planting. Before soaking the seeds, prepare them by scratching their surface, to allow the water to soak in. Next, prepare the land for planting. Clean the area of grass, and mix fertilizer and mud into the soil. Plan rows for the seeds, with a distance of 3m between each row. In each row, space seeds 20cm apart. Place seeds in the hole, cover with soil mixture, and water. Germination should occur within one week.

Pests and diseases: The white leadtree is not commonly susceptible to any pests or diseases.

Opposite page
Leucaena leucocephala
White leadtree flower

Right
Leucaena leucocephala
White leadtree

Uses: Trees in the *Leucaena* genus are used for a variety of purposes around the world. Their wood is used to make furniture. The leaves, flowers, fruits, and young fruit pods of these trees, when fresh, can be eaten as vegetables. The seeds of these trees are edible, and they are also used for medicinal, industrial, and ornamental purposes. In Africa and Asia, the seeds are toasted and grilled, then ground into coffee. In other areas, the seed pods and seeds are roasted and eaten. The seeds are high in protein, and as such are used as cattle fodder and in fertilizer. Medicinally, seed extracts have anthelmintic properties. In Sumatra and Indonesia, they are prescribed to expel parasitic worms from the body. The seeds are a natural charcoal source and, in the Caribbean, are strung together like beads to make necklaces.

Leucaena trees naturally improve the quality of the soil in which they are planted, through the decomposition of nitrogen-rich tissue. These trees are often planted in poor soil areas, where their constant shedding of leaves enriches the soil. They are also used as natural windbreaks for crops such as coffee and cocoa. When utilized for this purpose, farmers plant alternate lines of crop trees and *Leucaena* trees.

Above
Leucaena leucocephala
White leadtree
leaves and fruits

Melia azedarach
Chinaberry, Persian Lilac

Native to India and China, *Melia* is a genus of only three to five species of trees, including both deciduous and evergreen varieties. Plants in this genus are classified as shrubs or small trees.

***Melia azedarach*, chinaberry, Persian lilac:** The chinaberry is a many-branched, fast-growing deciduous tree, ranging in height from 10–15m and spreading to a width of between 5 and 8m. This dense, round-headed shade tree is nice in courtyards and large gardens, and is appropriate for the Gulf region, since it favors dry climates. It is, however, sensitive to sand and air pollution. *Melia azedarach* has fissured grey bark, and branches from which sprout alternate, pinnate or bi-pinnate leaves, approximately 35–40cm long. Each leaf is composed of narrow oval or scythe-shaped, mid- to bright green leaflets, with sharply toothed edges.

The chinaberry tree, also known as the Persian lilac, bears loose clusters of small, white, lilac or pale purple, honey-scented flowers. These tiny blossoms, only 2cm in diameter, bloom in arching pendant panicles, each 10–20cm long. As the flowers fade, bead-shaped to broadly ovoid berry-like fruits appear. These small berries are initially white, ripening to a yellow hue. The fruits, only 1cm in diameter, stay on the tree all winter, maturing to a wrinkled white. The berries are inedible and are in fact poisonous, though they are sometimes used for medicinal purposes. Each tiny fruit contains only one seed.

Care: *Melia azederach* trees thrive in full sun, and require placement in moderately fertile, well-drained soil. While these plants are drought tolerant, making them an excellent choice for Gulf gardens, they do need regular watering during the growing season, as well as a monthly application of liquid fertilizer. Chinaberry trees have messy growth habits, and benefit from regular pruning to maintain a pleasing shape.

Propagation: From seed. Chinaberry trees can also be propagated using cuttings, or by layering.

Pests and diseases: Plants in the genus *Melia* are susceptible to red spider mite damage. These pests should be treated by a licensed exterminator.

Uses: The chinaberry is a fragrant tree, and its aromatic leaves are one of its main points of usefulness. Farmers often plant chinaberry trees near barns and animal pens, where they act as a natural insecticide, keeping pests away from livestock. Dried chinaberry leaves can be placed in dressers, cupboards, or in books, to protect items from insects and bookworms. They can even be mixed with stored wheat, rice or corn to keep out weevils. *Melia* trees produce hardwood, which is often used as firewood, or in factories making furniture. Oil from chinaberry seeds is used in soaps and cosmetics, and the fruit is also used for medicinal purposes. In Asian countries, the tiny chinaberry seeds, once dried, are made into necklaces and prayer beads.

Opposite page
Melia azedarach
Chinaberry flowers

Right
Melia azedarach
Chinaberry fruits at various stages of growth and chinaberry tree

Millingtonia hortensis
Tree Jasmine, Indian Cork Tree

Native to South and South East Asia, from China to Malaysia, and common in countries such as Thailand and Myanmar, *Millingtonia* is a genus of only one species of fast-growing evergreen. Reaching a mature height of 18–25m and a spread of 11m in only six to eight years, this highly adaptable tree can survive in a variety of soils and climates, though it thrives in moist weather.

Millingtonia hortensis, tree jasmine, Indian cork tree: Commonly known as tree jasmine, *Millingtonia hortensis* has attractive foliage, and is striking with or without its blooms. The trunk of the tree is covered in deeply furrowed cork-like bark, and its wood is soft, yellowish-white, and brittle enough to break in a strong wind. The tree has an elongated pyramidal stem and slightly drooping branchlets. Each branchlet bears sets of opposite, bi-pinnate leaves, averaging 40cm in length. Each leaf is composed of ovate to lanceolate leaflets, 5–7cm long, with sinuate or crenate edges.

Millingtonia hortensis features large panicles of bell- or trumpet-shaped, waxy, white to greenish-yellow flowers. Each blossom has five small lobes, four stamens, and is bisexual, having both male and female organs. These fragrant flowers appear twice a year, from September to January, opening at night and in the early morning during cooler months. As the fragrant blooms fade and fall, they are followed by smooth, capsule-shaped fruits. Each fruit has two partitions, and contains broad-winged seeds. These fruits are a favorite of birds, and this is part of the plant's natural seed dispersal system.

Opposite page
Millingtonia hortensis
Tree jasmine flowers

Above
Millingtonia hortensis
Tree jasmine

Millingtonia hortensis can live for up to 40 years, in optimum conditions, and makes a perfect shade tree. It is also a good choice for under-planting.

Care: *Millingtonia hortensis* trees are a good addition to Gulf gardens because they are draught tolerant. Saplings should be placed in moderately fertile, well-drained soil in full sun. In the growing season, water freely and apply a balanced liquid fertilizer monthly. As they grow, these trees need regular pruning to maintain a pleasing shape.

Propagation: From seeds, seedlings, or cuttings. If propagating by seed, *Millingtonia hortensis* seeds must be sown immediately after the fruit ripens. Any delay drastically decreases the seed's viability.

Pests and diseases: *Millingtonia hortensis* is not commonly susceptible to pests and diseases.

Uses: Tree jasmine wood makes suitable timber, and the bark is sometimes used as an inferior form of cork. The leaves of *Millingtonia hortensis* can be dried and used as a substitute for tobacco, and an extract derived from the leaves has antimicrobial properties. The dried flowers of *Millingtonia hortensis* can be smoked for the treatment of asthma.

Opposite page
Millingtonia hortensis
Tree jasmine

Above
Millingtonia hortensis
Tree jasmine fruits, flowers and leaves

Mimusops elengi
Spanish Cherry

Native to tropical and subtropical regions of Asia, Africa, and Australia, as well as various oceanic islands, *Mimusops* is a genus of 40–45 species of ornamental, evergreen trees.

Mimusops elengi, **Spanish cherry:** Native to India and Sri Lanka, the Spanish cherry is a slow-growing evergreen. This small to medium-sized tree reaches a mature height of 9–20m. *Mimusops elengi* has a dense, rounded, leafy crown, spreading branches, and a short erect trunk. The trunk, which can measure up to 100cm in diameter, is often divided into several large main branches. It is covered with thick, dark, brownish-black or greyish-black bark, with striations and a few cracks on the surface.

The Spanish cherry tree features foliage composed of alternately or slightly spirally-arranged leaves which emerge at the ends of its branches. These leaves are simple, glossy, dark green in color and oblong elliptic or oval in shape, with wavy margins. They measure 5–16cm long, and 3–7cm wide.

Mimusops elengi flowers from March through July, producing small, hairy, bisexual blossoms. These flowers are cream or white in color, and have a crown rising from the center. They measure 1.2cm in diameter, bloom in clusters and have a corolla that forms a star-shaped ring when falling off. Spanish cherry blossoms are deeply fragrant flowers.

Mimusops elengi bears fruit in June, producing smooth, ovoid or oblong, softly hairy edible fruits. These fruits are pointed in shape, with eight distinct sepals at the base. Initially green, and ripening to an orange and finally bright-red hue, they have creamy yellow flesh. Each fruit has one or two blackish-brown seeds. Seeds measure up to 2cm long, are laterally compressed, and have a small circular basal scar. Spanish cherry fruits are a food source for birds and squirrels, and all parts of the plant exude a watery latex.

Opposite page and above
Mimusops elengi
Spanish cherry flowers

Above
Mimusops elengi
Spanish cherry

Spanish cherry trees are commonly planted by landscapers as an ornamental specimen or along roadsides, as they provide much-needed shade during the months from March to July. These trees fill the night air with the scent of their aromatic blossoms, and make a lovely addition to any garden.

Care: Trees in the *Mimusops* genus are drought resistant and thrive in full sunlight. This makes them a perfect choice for Arabian Gulf landscapes. For best results, plant trees in moderately fertile, well-drained soil.

Propagation: From seeds or cuttings. If propagating by seed, seeds should be sown directly into containers. Germination occurs anywhere from 17 to 82 days after planting, and seedlings can be transplanted once they are 20–30cm in height. *Mimusops* seeds can be stored for up to nine months after harvesting.

Pests and diseases: Plants in the *Mimusops* genus are particularly susceptible to fungal diseases. These afflictions should be treated by an experienced gardener.

Uses: Every part of the *Mimusops elengi* tree is useful, from its trunk to its seeds. Timber from the Spanish cherry is used as building material, and is also a source of fuel wood. The leaves have a variety of uses in traditional medicine; sap from the leaves is used to soothe sore eyes, boiled leaves are applied as cold compresses to treat headaches, and smoke from burnt leaves can be inhaled to treat ulcers in the nose. In India, the flowers of this tree are very popular. They are strung into garlands and used in perfumes, and a sweet-scented water distilled from them is used as a stimulant. Medicinally, the extract from the flowers is thought to treat heart disease. *Mimusops elengi* fruit is edible and is used in traditional medicine, and the seeds yield cooking oil.

In Ayurvedic medicine, a tonic made from the bark, flowers, fruits, and seeds of the *Mimusops elengi* plant is used in the treatment and maintenance of oral hygiene. Rinsing the mouth with it strengthens the teeth, prevents bad breath, and helps keep gums healthy.

Above
Mimusops elengi
Spanish cherry leaves and fruits

Moringa
Miracle Tree, Ben Tree

Native to tropical and subtropical regions throughout the world, *Moringa* is a genus of 13 species of plants. Members of the *Moringa* genus vary widely in size, ranging from tiny herbs to massive trees. *Moringa* plants are recognized as some of the most useful trees in Asia and Africa.

The following are the most common *Moringa* species grown in the Arabian Gulf region:

***Moringa oleifera*, drumstick tree, horseradish tree, miracle tree:** Native to Pakistan, Bangladesh, Afghanistan, and the Himalayan areas of India, *Moringa oleifera* is a fast-growing, open, erect tree which is deciduous. Known commonly as the drumstick tree, as well as by several other names, this majestic plant has an open crown of drooping, fragile branches, and reaches a mature height of 7–12m. Its crown is supported by a sturdy trunk, measuring up to 45cm in diameter, which is covered in cork-like bark. This bark is purplish- or greenish-white and hairy when the tree is young, fading to whitish-grey as the tree ages.

Moringa oleifera has foliage composed of bi-pinnate leaves, measuring up to 45cm in length. Each leaf consists of two rows of numerous, 6–8cm leaflets. This foliage serves as a backdrop for the tree's loose, slender, hairy, drooping clusters of creamy white, fragrant flowers. Emerging in springtime, each cluster of blossoms is 10–25cm long. The flowers are bisexual, and composed of five unequal, thinly veined petals. They measure 1–1.5cm in length and 2cm in width. *Moringa oleifera* flowers for the first time six months after planting, and will bloom thereafter at least twice a year, and sometimes year-round.

Drumstick trees produce fruit in the form of bean-like brown seedpods, about 20–45cm long. These pods are hanging, three-sided, and hold globular seeds measuring 1cm in diameter. The seeds have three whitish, papery wings, and are dispersed by wind and water. *Moringa oleifera* takes its common name, drumstick tree, from these long, slender, triangular seed-pods. It is also known as the horseradish tree, from the taste of its roots.

Opposite page
Moringa oleifera
Miracle tree flowers

Right
Moringa oleifera
Miracle tree

Moringa peregrina (synonym *Hyperanthera peregrina*), **Ben tree, wild drumstick tree:** Native to Egypt and the Arabian Peninsula from Saudi Arabia, Yemen, and Oman to the UAE, this fast-growing, deciduous, perennial tree grows to a mature height of 5–15m. Moringa is an erect tree with a thick main root and a trunk measuring 20–40cm in diameter, covered in corky bark. The bark may be grey, white, purple-grey or bright brown in color.

The branches and stem of the *Moringa peregrina* tree are brittle, and support foliage consisting of alternate, compound, bi-pinnate leaves, each 30–60cm long. The leaves are composed of two rows of numerous pale green, smooth leaflets. Ben trees bloom from March through May, producing loose, slender, drooping panicles of blossoms. Each panicle is 18–30cm long, and is composed of tiny, bisexual blooms, about 1–1.5cm long. The flowers have cream, white, or pink petals, and are sweetly scented.

Ben trees produce fruit in the form of elongated, capsule-shaped seedpods, about 30–50cm long. These pods are hanging, three-sided, and hold dark brown seeds. The seeds have three papery wings. *Moringa peregrina* takes its other common name, wild drumstick tree, from these long, slender, triangular seedpods.

Care: *Moringa* trees are a viable choice for Gulf gardens, as they thrive in full sun and are drought tolerant. They do, however, require monthly fertilization with a balanced liquid fertilizer, as well as frequent watering, during the growing season. *Moringa* trees need regular pruning after flowering, to maintain a pleasing shape and to avoid the formation of tight crotches between branches.

Propagation: From seed or from cuttings. When propagating by seed, *Moringa* seeds should be soaked in water up to 24 hours before planting.

Above
Moringa oleifera
Miracle tree leaves

Right
Moringa peregrina
Ben tree

Pests and diseases: Trees in the genus *Moringa* are susceptible to caterpillar, aphids, stem borer, and fruit fly damage. These pests should be treated by a licensed exterminator.

Uses: *Moringa oleifera* is sometimes called the Tree of Life or the Miracle Tree. Although one might think this was due to its medicinal uses, of which there are many, it is instead referring to its potential as a food source. *Moringa oleifera* can easily be termed one of the most nutritious plants on Earth. Every part of the tree is edible, as well as being very nutritious. The young seedpods and leaves of *Moringa oleifera* are used as vegetables. The leaves are the most nutritious part of the plant, being a significant source of B vitamins, vitamins A, C, D, E, and K, as well as a source of beta-carotene and essential elements such as manganese, calcium, iron, potassium and protein. The leaves are cooked and eaten like spinach, and can also be dried and crushed into a powder, which is then added to soups and sauces. The immature fruit of the *Moringa oleifera* tree are commonly consumed in South Asia; they are a good source of dietary fiber and magnesium. The seeds of the miracle tree can be prepared in several ways. Seeds from more mature pods can be eaten like peas or roasted like nuts; they contain high levels of vitamin C, and moderate amounts of vitamin B and dietary minerals. Mature seeds yield an edible oil, called ben oil, so named for its high concentration of behenic acid. This oil is similar in texture to olive oil. Even the roots of the *Moringa oleifera* are edible. They have a sharp flavor, and are usually shredded and used as a condiment.

Medicinally, consuming parts of the *Moringa oleifera* tree, in the form of capsules which can be purchased from pharmacies, has been shown to boost energy levels, improve digestion, stabilize mood, and aid immune system function. They protect the stomach lining, soothe stomach ulcers, and lower cholesterol and blood pressure. Some sources recommend taking four capsules daily for a noticeable increase in energy within three to four weeks. *Moringa* seeds are beneficial to lactating women, and have been shown to reduce swelling and increase breast milk production.

Above
Moringa peregrina
Ben tree flowers and fruits

Right
Moringa peregrina
Ben tree flowers

Moringa oleifera also has industrial, commercial, and environmental uses. The wood of this tree provides a pulp that is considered suitable for newsprint, wrapping paper, printing paper, and for viscose rayon-grade pulp for textiles and cellophane. Leaf powder derived from the foliage of this plant can be used as a soap for hand washing, and its seeds can be used for water purification. Environmentally, the roots of *Moringa oleifera* fix the soil surrounding the tree, and so this plant is used in areas where soil erosion is a problem.

Moringa peregrina is also valued. Cosmetically, a preparation made from the bark of this tree is thought to remove freckles. Industrially, the wood of this tree is a good source of fire-wood, charcoal, and building material. Commercially, the tree's foliage is sold as high-quality animal fodder. Medicinally, the leaves of *Moringa peregrina* are used traditionally as an analgesic, to treat abdominal pain, burns, constipation, and headache, as well as being a natural fever reducer. *Moringa peregrina* seed oil is a rich source of many essential nutrients that appear to have a very positive effect on health. The oil is extracted by boiling seeds with water and collecting the oil from the surface of the water. Oil from the seeds has been shown to be particularly effective in the manufacture of soap, producing a stable lather with high washing efficiency. This oil is also used in perfumes, hair care products, and as a machine lubricant. The seed cake remaining after the oil extraction process may be used as a fertilizer or as a flocculent to purify water. *Moringa* seed oil also has potential for use as a biofuel.

Moringa peregrina is potentially a very valuable tree. Due to the plant's high nutrient content, and the fact that the tree is tolerant to severe drought, the plant could become an important future crop in arid and semi-arid regions.

Above
Moringa peregrina
Ben tree leaves

Parkinsonia aculeata
Jerusalem Thorn

Native to the South-West region of the United States, as well as neighboring Central and South America and East Africa, *Parkinsonia* is a small genus of 12 species of deciduous evergreens. These shrubs or small trees average 2–10m in height.

***Parkinsonia aculeata*, Jerusalem thorn:** The Jerusalem thorn is a spreading, often weeping, tree. It is fast-growing, quickly reaching its mature height of 10m and spread of 5–8m. Jerusalem thorns can be cultivated as standard or multi-trunk trees. The trunk is covered in bark that is bright green when young, aging to a darker green-brown hue. The branches grow double or triple sharp spines, each about 7–12mm long, at the axils of the leaves. The foliage of this tree consists of leaves that are alternate, bi-pinnate, stalkless, mid-green, long, and slender, and often grow 15–30cm in length. Each leaf has two rows of 25–30 tiny oval to oblong leaflets, 2–5mm long, which give the foliage a feathery, fern-like appearance. These tiny leaflets are prone to dropping during dry conditions, and the petioles and twigs are green and photosynthetic.

Blooming in springtime, Jerusalem thorns produce loose clusters of two to 15 cup-shaped, fragrant, bright yellow-orange flowers. These pretty blossoms measure 2cm in diameter, with five sepals and five petals. Four of the petals are rhomboid ovate, while the fifth is elongated. The petals are orange-spotted at the base, and surround orange-red stamens. The flowers are pollinated by bees, and are followed by leathery seedpods, which turn a light brown color as they mature.

Jerusalem thorn trees make a lovely addition to parks and courtyards, or to the edge of patios. They are not appropriate for yard planting, however, as they do not do well with lawn watering.

Care: *Parkinsonia aculeata* trees are an appropriate choice for gardens in the Arabian Gulf region because they are drought tolerant. Plants should be placed in moderately fertile, well-drained soil in full sun. During the growing season, water freely and apply a balanced liquid fertilizer monthly. As they grow, these trees need regular pruning to maintain a balanced shape.

Propagation: From seed.

Pests and diseases: Trees in the *Parkinsonia* genus are susceptible to red spider mite damage. These pests should be treated by a licensed exterminator.

Uses: The wood of the Jerusalem thorn is used for firewood, charcoal, and is sometimes pulped for paper-making. In India, its leaves, twigs, and fruit pods are used as cattle fodder. The blossoms of this tree attract bees, which, in its native range, produce a fragrant honey from its flowers.

Opposite page
Parkinsonia aculeata
Jerusalem thorn flowers

Opposite page
Parkinsonia aculeata
Jerusalem thorn

Above
Parkinsonia aculeata
Jerusalem thorn fruits, trunk, leaves and thorns

Peltophorum pterocarpum
Yellow Flame Tree, Yellow Poinciana

Peltophorum is a small genus of five to seven species of evergreen trees. Originating in the Caribbean, South America, southern Africa, Southeast Asia and northern Australasia, plants in this genus reach an average height of 15–25m, and spread to a width of 8–10m.

Peltophorum pterocarpum, yellow flame tree, yellow flamboyant tree, yellow poinciana: *Peltophorum pterocarpum* is a fast-growing, wide-spreading, freely branching, deciduous tree native from tropical South East Asia to northern Australasia, but widely planted throughout the tropics and subtropics. It has a sturdy trunk, growing up to 1m in diameter, from which sprouts rust-red downy stems. Upon maturing these branches spread to form an umbrella-like crown. This stately tree grows to a maximum height of 25m, and a width of 8–10m. The foliage of the flame tree is composed of large, alternate, bi-pinnate, deep green leaves. These leaves, growing 30–60cm in length, are made of eight to 20 pairs of pinnae, with each pinna consisting of 20–40 oval-elliptic-oblong leaflets. These delicate leaflets are 2cm long.

The yellow flame tree, also known as the yellow flamboyant tree, gets its second common name from its striking ascending racemes, or panicles, of fragrant, bright yellow flowers. These flowers, blossoming in summer, form at the tree's uppermost leaf axils. Each panicle measures 45cm long and each flower measures 4cm across, with five obovate, crinkly or frilled petals, each with a central brownish red mark. These beautiful blooms are followed by elliptic to oblong, winged, purple-brown seedpods. Each pod is 8–10cm long, and contains one to four seeds.

Peltophorum pterocarpum trees flower for the first time approximately four years after planting. These trees are often sown in gardens as specimen plants, and are occasionally used in street landscaping in tropical regions.

Care: Yellow poinciana trees are a beautiful way to add color to Gulf gardens, as they thrive in full sun and tolerate dry climates. However, they require moist but well-drained soil, and should be pruned at least once a year.

Propagation: From seed. Seeds must be pre-soaked. To prepare seeds, scratch the surface of the seed pod to allow it to soak up water, place in soil, and allow to germinate at a maintained temperature of 18–21°C.

Pests and diseases: Trees in the *Peltophorum* genus are susceptible to red spider mite and whitefly damage. These pests should be treated by a licensed exterminator.

Uses: Wood from the trunk of the yellow flame tree is used in the manufacturing of cabinets, and the leaves are used as livestock fodder.

Opposite page
Peltophorum pterocarpum
Yellow flame tree flowers

Opposite page
Peltophorum pterocarpum
Yellow flame tree flowers

Above
Peltophorum pterocarpum
Yellow flame tree flower, leaves and fruits

Platycladus orientalis
Oriental Thuja

Platycladus is a genus containing only one distinct species of evergreen tree. Native to China, Korea and the Russian Far East, and naturalized across much of central Asia from Japan as far west as Iran, this conical or irregularly crowned, monoecious, coniferous tree grows to heights ranging from 3–20m, and spreads to a width of 2–6m.

***Platycladus orientalis* (synonym *Thuja orientalis*), oriental thuja:** Commonly known as oriental thuja, this tree has a fibrous trunk covered in red-brown bark, which supports erect, irregularly arranged, flattened sprays of scale-like, wedge- or diamond-shaped leaves. These blunt-tipped leaves, growing in two ranks of opposite pairs, average 2–3mm in length. They release a strong aromatic scent when bruised, and are initially mid- or yellow-green in color, turning bronze in winter. This tree produces small, erect, ovoid to pear-shaped, grey-hued female cones. These cones measure 2cm in length and have three or four pairs of scales. Each scale has a prominent reflexed hook just below its tip. The male cones of the *Platycladus orientalis* tree are only 1mm long and ovoid in shape.

There are many cultivars of this plant, some dwarf or slow-growing, and these varieties are attractive when planted in containers or rock gardens, or developed as bonsai. Oriental thuja are often used in landscaping, at the entrance of a yard or as a natural privacy fence around swimming pools. For barriers or hedging, these trees should be planted 2–3m apart.

Caution: Care should be taken as contact with *Platycladus orientalis* foliage may aggravate skin allergies.

Care: Oriental thuja is a wonderful addition to gardens in the Arabian Gulf, as it tolerates dry weather and thrives in full sun. It does require well-drained soil, however, and should be trimmed at least twice a year, in spring and late summer.

Propagation: From seed, or by rooting semi-ripe cuttings.

Pests and diseases: *Platycladus orientalis* trees are susceptible to aphid damage. These pests should be treated by a licensed exterminator.

Opposite page
Platycladus orientalis
Oriental thuja flowers

Opposite page
Platycladus orientalis
Oriental thuja

Above
Platycladus orientalis
Oriental thuja flowers and fruits

Plumeria
Frangipani

Native to tropical and subtropical regions of the Americas, *Plumeria* is a small genus of only four species of deciduous or evergreen shrubs and trees. Colloquially known as frangipani, trees in this genus range in height from 4–7m, and spread to a width of 2–5m. They have succulent stems, thick, fleshy branches, and simple, entire leaves, which are clustered at the tip of their stems and are alternately or spirally arranged. *Plumeria* trees produce terminal clusters or panicles of fragrant, salverform flowers. Each blossom has five broad petal lobes, and emerges on bare stems or with young leaves.

Frangipani are typically grown as specimen plants, and dwarf varieties are popular for use in containers. These plants require plentiful sunlight and well-drained soil to thrive. Mature frangipani trees acquire a round shape and overall ample girth, and so should be planted in a spacious area of the garden.

The following are the most common *Plumeria* species grown in the Arabian Gulf region:

Plumeria alba, white frangipani: *Plumeria alba*, also known as white frangipani, is a medium-sized tree in the *Plumeria* genus, growing to a mature height of 6m and spreading 4m wide. This tree features a robust, thick trunk and spirally arranged, lance-shaped, slightly wrinkled, round-ended leaves. Each rich green leaf grows about

Opposite page
Plumeria rubra
Common frangipani flowers and leaves

Above
Plumeria alba
White frangipani flowers

Above
Plumeria alba
White frangipani

30cm long, and is usually finely-haired on the underside. *Plumeria alba* produces terminal panicles of five-petalled, salverform, yellow-eyed, creamy white, fragrant blossoms. These flowers, measuring 6cm in diameter, bloom from summer through to autumn.

***Plumeria rubra*, common frangipani:** Common frangipani is classified in size as a small tree or large shrub, growing to a maximum height of 7m and width of 5m. This deciduous, upright, sparsely branched tree has foliage consisting of very thick stems bearing alternately arranged, broadly elliptic to oblong or inversely lance-shaped leaves. Each leaf is 20–40cm long, glossy mid-green in color, with paler mid-ribs, and has a pointed end. The underside of the plant's leaves may be hairy. *Plumeria rubra* bears terminal panicles of five-petalled, salverform, fragrant flowers, measuring 7–10cm in diameter. These blossoms are usually rose-pink or occasionally yellow or red to bronze in color, with yellow eyes, and bloom from summer through to autumn.

Caution: The milky sap emitted by this tree may cause mild stomach upset if ingested.

Care: *Plumeria* trees are a colorful addition to any landscape, and fit perfectly in the Gulf as they thrive in full sun and tolerate dry climates. During the growing season these trees should be watered freely and receive a monthly application of a balanced liquid fertilizer. Frangipani plants require moist, well-drained soil and pruning once a year to truly flourish.

Propagation: Plants in the *Plumeria* genus can be propagated from seed, but they also root very easily from cuttings. Take a cutting approximately 30cm long, making sure to leave some of the old wood on it. Allow the cutting to heal in a dry location for one week, and then plant in a free-draining propagating mix. Water sparingly to avoid rot.

Pests and diseases: Frangipani trees are susceptible to rust fungus. This disease should be treated by an experienced gardener.

Above
Plumeria alba
White frangipani flowers and leaves

Above
Plumeria rubra
Common frangipani

Above
Plumeria sp.
Frangipani flowers

Polyalthia longifolia
False Ashoka Tree, Indian Mast Tree

Native to Africa, Asia, Australia, and the Pacific Islands, *Polyalthia* is a genus of 80–100 species of evergreen trees.

Polyalthia longifolia, false ashoka tree, Indian mast tree: A fast-growing, evergreen tree from India and Sri Lanka, *Polyalthia longifolia* is sometimes incorrectly identified as the ashoka tree (*Saraca indica*) because of their close resemblance. This stately tree grows to a mature height of 10–20m, and spreads to a width of 2–7m. It is symmetrically pyramidal in shape, with a straight, slender trunk covered in grey bark. This trunk supports a dense crown of drooping branches. The false ashoka has foliage consisting of simple, alternate, lanceolate leaves with wavy edges and a short petiole. New leaves are a coppery brown color and are soft and delicate to the touch. As the leaves grow older they turn light green, and finally mature to a glossy dark green hue with lighter mid-veins and undersides.

Polyalthia longifolia blooms in spring or early summer, producing inconspicuous, delicate blossoms with five narrowly triangular, star-like pale green petals. These tiny flowers are

Opposite page
Polyalthia longifolia
False ashoka tree flowers

Above
Polyalthia longifolia
False ashoka tree
and leaves

Right
Polyalthia longifolia
False ashoka tree

arranged in pendulous racemes or umbels, and tend to blend in with the foliage. The flowers last for a short period, usually two to three weeks, and are followed by clusters of 10–20 small, spherical fruit. Fruits are initially green, turning purple or black when ripe, and contain only one seed. False ashoka trees attract bees and butterflies, and their fruits are eaten by birds and bats.

Care: *Polyalthia longifolia* trees thrive in full sun or partial shade and can tolerate dry conditions, perfect for the Gulf region. However, they do require some specialized care. Plant trees in well-drained soil and ensure regular irrigation. Fertilize three times a year, in spring, summer, and autumn, with a top-quality granular fertilizer. This tree does not need pruning, as the plant's natural shape lends to its beauty.

Propagation: From seed, using softwood cuttings, or by air layering. If propagating by seed, sow seeds directly outdoors into the garden.

Pests and diseases: *Polyalthia longifolia* leaves are a favorite food of the larva of Kite swallowtail butterflies. These pests should be treated by a licensed exterminator.

Uses: The false ashoka gets its other common name, Indian mast tree, from the building of sailing ships. In the past the lightweight, flexible wood of the trees' tall trunks was used to create masts. Today, timber from the trunk of the tree is mostly used for manufacturing small articles such as pencil boxes. The bark of the false ashoka is a source of fiber, and is used in traditional Indian medicine to treat fever, skin diseases, hypertension, and helmintheasis. The leaves of *Polyalthia longifolia* are used in India for ornamental decorations and in cultural festivals.

The false ashoka is a staple of landscapers on the Indian subcontinent. The tree can be trimmed into various shapes and sizes, and as such is popular as a park and garden plant. *Polyalthia longifolia* trees are particularly attractive when planted in rows, and are surprisingly wind-tolerant, making them effective windbreaks. They are also planted as hedges for privacy and to reduce noise pollution.

Pongamia pinnata
Poona Oil Tree

Pongamia is a genus of only one distinct species of wide-spreading, deciduous or semi-evergreen tree. Native to Malaysia, Indonesia and Northern Australasia/Oceania, this fast-growing tree quickly reaches its mature height of 20–25m and width of 15–25m.

Pongamia pinnata, poona oil tree: Popular in tropical and coastal areas as a windbreak or shade tree, the poona oil tree features a large domed canopy and a short, straight or crooked trunk. This trunk, covered in grey-brown bark and averaging 50–80cm in diameter, may be smooth or marred by vertical fissures. Poona oil trees feature attractive, tender soft pink-bronze foliage, which darkens as it matures to a glossy green hue. The alternate leaves are short-stalked and pinnate, with prominent veins underneath. Each leaf is rounded or cuneate at the base, obtuse or pointed at the apex, and composed of five to nine ovate leaflets. The leaves range from 15–30cm in length.

Pongamia pinnata begins flowering the summer or autumn of its third or fourth year of growth. This tree features axillary racemes, 13cm long, of showy, pea-like, white, purple or mauve-pink flowers. These blossoms, each 1.5cm in diameter, have a bell-shaped calyx and rounded, ovate petals with basal auricles. In the center of each bloom is an eye-catching spot of green. Poona oil flowers are fragrant, particularly when crushed.

Immediately after the flowers fade, the tree's brown seedpods appear. These pods are thick-walled, smooth, and somewhat flattened and elliptical in shape, slightly rounded with a short, curved point. Each pod contains one or two bean-like brownish-red seeds. Each seed is 1.5–2.5cm long, weighs 1.1–1.8g, and has a brittle, oily coat. The seedpods take approximately 10–11 months to mature, and do not split open naturally; rather, the pods must first decompose before seeds can germinate. Commercially, the seeds are harvested in the spring, with each tree yielding 10–50kg of seeds per season.

Care: *Pongamia pinnata* trees must be planted in well-drained soil, in an area of the garden that receives full sunlight. While these trees

Opposite page and above
Pongamia pinnata
Poona oil tree flowers

Above
Pongamia pinnata
Poona oil tree

tolerate dry conditions, they should be watered freely during the growing season. At this time of year, they also require a monthly application of a balanced liquid fertilizer. Poona oil trees need yearly pruning to remove old growth and maintain a pleasing shape.

Propagation: From seed. Poona oil seeds must be prepared before planting. Cover seeds with water and allow to soak overnight. Plant seeds in a well-drained potting mix, and place in a location receiving partial or full sunlight. Seeds should germinate within three to 10 days. *Pongamia pinnata* can also be propagated in summer by rooting semi-ripe cuttings.

Pests and diseases: The poona oil tree is susceptible to whitefly damage. These pests should be treated by a licensed exterminator.

Uses: Poona oil trees are an excellent choice for gardens with poor soil quality, as the tree is nitrogen fixing, moving nutrients from the air into the soil. Its leaves are leguminous, and they enrich the soil with nitrogen as they fall and decompose. The leaves are a good source of green manure, and the flowers are also nutrient rich and often used as plant compost. The bark of the poona oil tree is pliable and can be used to make twine or rope. It produces a black gum which has been used in traditional medicine to treat wounds caused by poisonous fish. The fruits, sprouts, and seeds of this tree are also used in many traditional remedies.

Pongamia pinnata trees are perhaps best known for the oil produced from their seeds. Between 30% and 42% of the composition of each seed is a yellowish-orange to brown colored oil, commonly known as pongam oil. Pongam oil has both industrial and medicinal uses. It is used as lamp oil, in leather tanning, and in soap making. It can be used to power diesel generators, and is now being explored as an alternate fuel source, or biofuel. Pongam oil is a natural insecticide, as well as an antiseptic. It is toxic if ingested, and will induce nausea and vomiting; it is, however, still used in traditional medicine. The by-products of the pongam oil extraction process contain up to 30% protein, and this material is sometimes used as a feed supplement for livestock.

Above
Pongamia pinnata
Poona oil tree
fruits and leaves

Prosopis
Ghaf Tree, Mesquite

Prosopis is a genus of 45 species of evergreen plants. These fine-leafed shrubs and trees thrive in hot sun and are salt-tolerant. They are one of the few shade-providing trees of the desert.

The following are the most common *Prosopis* species grown in the Arabian Gulf region:

Prosopis cineraria, ghaf tree: The species *Prosopis cineraria* is native to South West Asia, including the Arabian Gulf countries. It is a slow-growing, elegant tree with a rounded canopy that once mature bears slender, drooping branches. The ghaf is petite, ranging only 3–9m in height, making it ideal for smaller gardens and courtyard plantings. Care should be taken, however, as the branches bear short thorns along their length. This plant has foliage consisting of bi-pinnate leaves, 1–5cm long, bearing one to three pairs of pinnae, each having seven to 14 pairs of leaflets. Its flowers are creamy yellow, very small, and borne in spikes 5–20cm long. Ghaf trees produce pale yellow seedpods, 10–25cm in length and 4–8mm wide, each containing 10–25 dark brown seeds.

Prosopis juliflora, mesquite: A fast-growing, wide-spreading, leguminous shrub or small tree, the mesquite plant is native to Mexico and is commonly found in arid and semi-arid regions. It is very successful and is invasive and considered a notifiable weed in some countries. It thrives in these harsh conditions due to its well-developed lateral roots and its taproot, which grows down many meters in search of water. Reaching a mature height of 3–15m and a width of 12–15m, this airy, heavily branched tree features an attractive umbrella-shaped crown. Its sturdy trunk, reaching a girth of up to 1.5m, is covered in thick, rough, grey-green bark that becomes scaly with age. The trunk supports branches from which sprout drooping, green-brown stems. These twisted, flexible stems have long, strong thorns, measuring as much as 1.5–5cm in length. *Prosopis juliflora* has foliage consisting of bi-pinnate leaves, 6–8cm long, bearing 12–20 pairs of small, linear, oblong leaflets. Mesquite foliage is bright emerald green in early spring, fading to a bluish-green in summer. It serves as a colorful backdrop for the tree's tiny, fragrant, yellow or yellowish-green flowers. Blossoms grow in clusters of two to five at the ends of the tree's branches, borne in sparse, hanging, cylindrical spikes 5–10cm long.

Prosopis juliflora blooms in springtime, and goes on to bear fruit in the form of flat, curled, pale yellow seedpods. These pods are 10–30cm long, and contain between 10 and 20 hard, oval or elliptic seeds per pod. Trees first produce fruit three years after planting, and a mature mesquite tree can produce hundreds of thousands of seeds. These seeds remain viable for up to 10 years.

Care: Trees in the *Prosopis* genus thrive in warm locations with full sunlight; they are sensitive to cold weather and frost. They are drought tolerant, although droughts during flowering periods may affect flower and seedpod production. *Prosopis* trees are low maintenance, requiring pruning only once a year.

Propagation: From seed.

Pests and diseases: Trees in the genus *Prosopis* are not commonly susceptible to pests or diseases.

Opposite page
Prosopis juliflora
Mesquite flowers

Uses: Various parts of both the mesquite and ghaf trees serve industrial and environmental purposes, as well as being food sources. In some Gulf states, the conservation of the ghaf tree is encouraged; people are urged to plant it in their gardens to combat desertification and to preserve their country's heritage. Although the wood and other parts of the ghaf tree serve a variety of purposes, it is very nutritious and has traditionally been used to provide fodder for grazing animals. Ghaf wood is insect and drought tolerant, and as such has been used in the past as an excellent material for furniture production. Historically, this wood was also used as roof beams in houses throughout the Middle East.

Due to their high tolerance for heat, salt, and sand, ghaf trees are often planted in desert areas to prevent soil erosion. As they shed their leaves, faded flowers, and spent fruit, the nitrogen-rich droppings of *Prosopis cineraria* enhance the quality of the soil wherever planted.

The mesquite tree is probably best known for its use as a high-quality charcoal, famous for flavoring barbecued meat. However, this plant has other uses. Its stems contain a gum similar to gum arabic. In Central America, numerous food preparations are made out of *Prosopis juliflora*, including bread, syrup, sweets and sweeteners, alcoholic beverages and a drink similar to coffee. In fact, the mesquite tree was one of the earliest legume foods used by humans.

Opposite page
Prosopis cineraria
Ghaf trees, fruits and flowers

Above
Prosopis juliflora
Mesquite tree, leaves and fruits

Schinus
Pepper Tree

Schinus is a genus of 30 species of deciduous or evergreen trees and shrubs. Native to tropical and subtropical regions of South America, these perennial plants feature foliage consisting of alternate leaves, which may be simple or pinnate, entire or toothed. When in flower, trees in the *Schinus* genus produce tiny, four- or five-petalled blossoms borne in terminal or axillary panicles. When plants of both sexes are grown together, the flowers on female plants are followed by small, red to purple fruits.

The following are the most common *Schinus* species grown in the Arabian Gulf region:

Schinus molle, American pepper tree: Native to Mexico, Brazil, Bolivia, Chile, Peru, Uruguay, and Argentina, *Schinus molle* is an erect, evergreen tree. Commonly known as the American pepper, this fast growing, medium- to large-sized tree ranges from 10–25m in height, depending on the climate, making it the largest of all *Schinus* species. It is also potentially the longest-lived plant in the *Schinus* genus.

The twisted trunk of the American pepper tree is covered in rough greyish bark, and drips sap. It supports a round spreading crown, 3–5m wide, composed of slender, pendent branches which are glaucous when young. *Schinus molle* has foliage consisting of arching or semi-pendent, pinnate leaves, 10–30cm long. Each leaf is composed of 19–41 narrow, lance-shaped, toothed, glossy, mid- to deep green leaflets, measuring 5cm in length.

The American pepper tree is dioecious, with male and female flowers occurring on separate plants. From late winter through summer, blooms emerge in pendent panicles, 8–20cm long, at the ends of drooping branches. Each tiny blossom has five whitish yellow petals. Spent flowers give way to globose, shiny, rose-pink fruit. These tiny fruit are drupes, with a solitary woody seed, and measure only 6–7mm in diameter.

Schinus terebinthifolius, Brazilian pepper tree: A small tree with erect to spreading stems, the Brazilian pepper is native to Paraguay, Argentina, and Brazil, but widely grown in many parts of the tropics. *Schinus terebinthifolius* reaches a mature height of 5–10m, and features a round-headed to umbrella-shaped crown that

Opposite page
Schinus molle
American pepper tree flowers

Above
Schinus molle
American pepper tree leaves and fruits

Above
Schinus terebinthifolius
Brazilian pepper tree

spreads to a width of 3–5m. The foliage of this tree consists of pinnate, elliptical leaves, 10–17cm long, with winged midribs. Each leaf is composed of oblong leaflets, deep green on top and paler beneath. Most leaves have an average of seven leaflets, but they can range from three to 13 in number. Brazilian pepper trees flower from summer to autumn, producing panicles of tiny white flowers. These panicles can measure up to 15cm in length, and are followed by bright red fruit.

Caution: Contact with Brazilian pepper tree seeds may irritate skin and cause respiratory problems.

Care: *Schinus* trees are hardy and low-maintenance; they need only be pruned once a year. During the growing season they should be watered regularly and receive a monthly application of a balanced liquid fertilizer. *Schinus* trees can be planted in any area of the garden that is dry, has well-drained soil, and receives full sun.

Propagation: Pepper trees can be propagated by seed year-round, by air layering in the spring, or by rooting semi-ripe cuttings in the summer.

Pests and diseases: Plants in the *Schinus* genus are susceptible to scale insect and red spider mite damage. These pests should be treated by a licensed exterminator.

Uses: Various parts of the *Schinus molle* tree serve industrial, medicinal, and culinary purposes. Extracts from the plant have been used as a flavor in drinks and syrups. The bark, leaves, and fruit are strongly aromatic when crushed. This tree has insecticidal properties, and has been considered as an alternative to synthetic chemicals in pest control. The leaves are also used for the natural dying of textiles in the Andean region. Medicinally, *Schinus molle* has been used in traditional remedies for a variety of ailments including toothache, rheumatism, and menstrual disorders, and is known to be both an antidepressant and a diuretic. Topically, due to its antibacterial properties, parts of the tree have been used to treat wounds and infections.

For landscaping purposes, both the American and Brazilian pepper trees make an excellent focal point for large gardens. However, both species produce debris. To reduce the possibility of wind damage, shorten overlong horizontal branches and thin the interior of the tree periodically to allow the wind to pass through. *Schinus terebinthifolius* is a good street tree, when grown as a single-trunk specimen, or in parks, when allowed to flourish as a wide-spreading multi-trunk tree. *Schinus molle* can be planted in clusters as a privacy screen for the garden in the form of a shrub border or large hedge.

Above
Schinus terebinthifolius
Brazilian pepper tree fruits and leaves

Senna
Golden Senna, Empress Candle Plant

Native to South America, Africa, Asia, and Australia, *Senna* is a large genus of 206 species of deciduous or evergreen perennial herbs, trees, and shrubs. Plants in the *Senna* genus feature foliage consisting of alternate and pinnately compound leaves, with linear to nearly rounded leaflets. They are often planted for their lovely yellow or rarely white, pea-like blossoms, which emerge in terminal or axillary racemes, corymbs, or long panicles. These flowers are followed by often flattened, pea-like seedpods.

The following are the most common *Senna* species grown in the Arabian Gulf region:

Senna alata (synonym *Cassia alata*), empress candle plant: *Senna alata*, or the empress candle plant, is an erect to spreading evergreen, native to tropical America but widely grown elsewhere. This small to medium-sized shrub or tree ranges from 2–10m in height, depending on the climate, and spreads to a width of 2–5m. *Senna alata* has broadly oblong to obovate, pinnate leaves, each 20–75cm in length. These leaves are composed of six to 14 pairs of oblong, obtuse leaflets. This foliage provides a contrast for the tree's bright yellow flowers. These blossoms, measuring 2.5cm in diameter, grow in erect, axillary racemes of 14–28 flowers. The blooms are protected by broad, yellowish-green bracts below each bud.

Senna surattensis (synonym *Cassia surattensis*), golden senna, scrambled egg tree: Native to Southeast Asia, India, and tropical Australia, *Senna surattensis* is a small, semi-deciduous,

Opposite page
Senna surattensis
Golden senna flowers

Above
Senna surattensis
Golden senna

fast-growing evergreen with a dense, round crown and a short trunk covered by smooth, grey bark. This tree has a shallow root system, which can easily be uprooted by strong winds. *Senna surattensis* reaches a height of 3–6m, and spreads to a maximum width of 7m. This tree has an open habit and hairless young stems from which grow pinnate, dark green or deep yellowish-green leaves, each 8–18cm in length. Each leaf is composed of 6–10 pairs of oblong-lance-shaped leaflets, ranging from 2–5cm long and 80mm to 2cm wide.

The *Senna surattensis* tree blooms from spring through to summer, producing dense, erect, terminal, corymb-like panicles of flowers, each 2cm in diameter. These panicles grow up to 60cm long, and hold between 10 and 60 blossoms. It is these bright yellow blooms that give the plant its common name, the scrambled egg tree. As the flowers fade they are followed by soft, flat, brown seedpods, about 15–25cm long, containing three to five seeds per pod. These seeds are bean-shaped, shiny dark-brown, and measure 8mm in length. Golden senna is often planted as a landscape tree along streets and in other public spaces.

Care: *Senna* trees are a colorful addition to any landscape, and fit perfectly in the Gulf as they thrive in full sun and tolerate dry climates. During the growing season these trees should be watered freely and receive a monthly application of a balanced liquid fertilizer. *Senna* plants require moist, well-drained soil and pruning once a year to truly flourish.

Propagation: By seed. Plants in the *Senna* genus can also be propagated through division of perennials, or by rooting semi-ripe cuttings. *Senna* trees should be cultivated with caution, however, as many *Senna* species can become invasive weeds if there is an ample water supply. Regular weeding of spontaneous seedlings is recommended.

Pests and diseases: Trees in the *Senna* genus are susceptible to caterpillars. These pests should be treated by a licensed exterminator.

Opposite page
Senna surattensis
Golden senna

Above
Senna surattensis
Golden senna
fruits and leaves

Uses: The leaves and sap of *Senna* trees have anti-fungal properties, and as such are used to treat a wide variety of skin afflictions. The leaves may be boiled and left to simmer in water, and this liquid can be applied twice a day to open wounds to facilitate healing. For ringworm, eczema, and other fungal infections of the skin, the leaves are ground in a mortar to obtain a kind of green cotton wool. This substance is mixed with an equal amount of vegetable oil and rubbed on the affected area two to three times a day. Leaf decoctions from *Senna* plants are also used to treat skin conditions in livestock, as well as being used as a natural insecticide to protect against external parasites such as mites and ticks.

Of the many plants in the *Senna* genus, *Senna alata* is popular for its wide variety of uses. Aside from being a beautiful addition to the garden, this tree serves as a common forage for bees. Its leaves, once toasted, are sometimes ground as a coffee substitute, and products from the bark of this tree are used as fish poison and for tanning leather. Dye derived from the bark and roots of the tree has been used in tattooing, and the seeds are a source of gum.

Perhaps the most commonly known use of *Senna* plants is that of *Senna alata* as a laxative or purgative. For the treatment of constipation or other stomach ailments, a tea is made from boiling the leaves (or, less often, the flowers, stems, and roots) of the plant.

In some areas of the world, various parts of the *Senna alata* tree are used in traditional medicine and for cosmetic purposes. Due to its anti-fungal properties, it is a common ingredient in soaps, shampoos, and lotions in the Philippines. In Africa, the boiled leaves are used to treat high-blood pressure. In South America, this decoction is also used to treat a wide range of ailments from stomach problems, fever, and asthma, to snake bites and venereal diseases such as syphilis and gonorrhea. Decoctions of the wood are also used to treat liver problems.

Opposite page
Senna alata
Empress candle plant

Above
Senna alata
Empress candle plant flower and fruit

Spathodea campanulata
African Tulip Tree

Spathodea is a genus of only one species, *Spathodea campanulata*, commonly known as the African tulip tree. Native to tropical Africa, this upright, open, leafy-branched evergreen grows to a height of 18–25m and spreads to a width of 10–18m.

Spathodea campanulata, African tulip tree: *Spathodea campanulata* features foliage consisting of opposite, pinnate leaves, each about 45cm long, composed of nine to 19 oblong to ovate, leathery leaflets. These deep green leaves serve as the perfect contrast for the tree's main attraction, its large, dramatic, tulip-shaped, orange-red or occasionally pure yellow flowers. The flowers begin as ampoule-shaped buds, containing water. These buds are a favorite of children, because when they are compressed the water squirts out. Care should be taken, however, as sap from the flowers can stain fingers and clothing yellow. African tulip blossoms, measuring up to 7cm in diameter, bloom several times a year, emerging in racemes at the end of the tree's upper branches. The open flowers hold rain and dew, attracting

Opposite page
Spathodea campanulata
African tulip tree flowers

Above
Spathodea campanulata
African tulip tree
and fruits

Right
Spathodea campanulata
African tulip tree

birds to the tree. Each flower lasts for several days before it falls and is replaced by another, and the same inflorescence may continue this cycle for a month or more. The flowers are followed by long, boat-shaped seedpods which split open to release winged seeds.

Spathodea campanulata is a fast-growing tree, experiencing as much as 2m of upward growth per year. This rapid growth means the wood of the tree is soft and brittle. While this makes the tree a favorite of birds who build nests by making holes in its trunk, it also means that its branches are likely to break in high winds, making it unsuitable for planting near houses or other buildings. African tulip trees thrive in full sun, making them a perfect addition to gardens in the Arabian Gulf region.

Care: *Spathodea* trees must be planted in well-drained soil, in an area of the garden that receives full sunlight. While these trees tolerate dry conditions, they should be watered freely during the growing season. At this time of year they also require a monthly application of a balanced liquid fertilizer. African tulip trees need yearly pruning to remove old growth and maintain a pleasing shape.

Propagation: *Spathodea campanulata* trees are most successfully propagated using root cuttings. Seed fertility is inconsistent, although this species has become invasive through self-seeding in several high humidity tropical countries. However, due to lack of water, it is unlikely to self-seed successfully in the Gulf region.

Pests and diseases: *Spathodea campanulata* trees are susceptible to red spider mite damage. These pests should be treated by a licensed exterminator.

Uses: Various parts of *Spathodea campanulata* are used in its native Africa for medicinal purposes. The bark has laxative and antiseptic properties. It may also be boiled in water, which is then used for bathing newborns to heal body rashes. In addition to the bark, the flowers and roots are also used as medicine. The seeds are edible, and the tree's soft, light brownish-white wood is used for carving and making drums. The most toxic part of the tree, the hard central portion of the fruit, is used as a natural exterminating agent for pests, and is also used by native hunters.

Above
Spathodea campanulata
African tulip tree
flowers and buds

Tabebuia
Trumpet Tree

Native to countries throughout Central and South America, *Tabebuia* is a genus of about 75 species of fast growing, deciduous trees and shrubs. These trees range between 12 and 25m in height, and spread 10–20m wide. They have foliage consisting of opposite, long-stalked, palmate, simple or fully divided, palmately three to seven-foliate leaves. They also produce terminal panicles of striking three- to five-lobed, tubular to trumpet or bell-shaped flowers, usually blooming in springtime. *Tabebuia* trees are grown primarily for this attractive display.

Plants in the *Tabebuia* genus, commonly known as trumpet trees, are used by gardeners as patio, specimen or lawn trees, and can even be placed in containers while young. Some species of *Tabebuia*, particularly *Tabebuia aurea*, are grown as bonsai. Trees in this genus are tolerant to salty spray, and are often used in landscaping along public streets in coastal environments. These plants are messy, however, and spent leaves and flowers will cover the ground surrounding the tree.

The following are the most common *Tabebuia* species grown in the Arabian Gulf region:

***Tabebuia aurea* (synonyms *Tabebuia argentea*, *Tabebuia caraiba*), silver trumpet tree, yellow trumpet tree:** *Tabebuia aurea* is a species of the dry-deciduous forest. The trunks of these trees, slender and covered in grey or silvery bark, are topped by an open crown, with two or three major trunks or branches dominating the crown. Reaching a height of 7–12m, this tree

Opposite page
Tabebuia aurea
Yellow trumpet tree flowers

Above
Tabebuia aurea
Yellow trumpet tree

has silvery-grey, leathery, palmately compound leaves, composed of five to seven narrow and elongated leaflets. The leaflets are silvery on their underside. *Tabebuia aurea* usually flowers after its leaves have fallen, leaving a dramatic display of color. Indicative of its common name, the yellow trumpet tree features yellow, trumpet-shaped flowers, each about 8cm long, growing in dense clusters towards the ends of its branches. As the flowers fade they are followed by glabrous, linear, bean-like, capsule-shaped fruits, about 9–10cm long and 2.5cm wide, containing winged seeds.

Tabebuia rosea, rosy trumpet tree: *Tabebuia rosea*, the rosy trumpet tree or pink poui, is an upright, deciduous tree, reaching heights of 20–25m and spreading to a width of 10–15m. These trees have long, smooth trunks, branching near the top, and long-stalked, palmately compound leaves. Each leaf is made up of five oblong to ovate-elliptic, leathery, scaly, mid- to dark green leaflets. The central leaflet is longer than the others, growing to a length of 25–30cm. *Tabebuia rosea* blossoms after its leaves have fallen, at the end of the dry season, producing vivid blooms of funnel-shaped, yellow-eyed, white, pink, or lilac flowers. Each flower is 5–10cm long, growing in pairs in dense panicles.

Care: Trumpet trees are perfect additions to gardens in the Gulf region, as they do well in sandy soil, are drought tolerant, and thrive in full sun. Care must be taken, however, to water new trees regularly for several weeks after planting.

Propagation: Trees in the *Tabebuia* genus can be propagated by seed, air layering, or by rooting semi-ripe stem cuttings. If propagating by seed, remove seeds as soon as pods crack open and sow within one to two weeks. This will ensure successful germination.

Opposite page
Tabebuia aurea
Yellow trumpet tree

Above
Tabebuia aurea
Yellow trumpet tree
leaves and fruit

Right
Tabebuia rosea
Rosy trumpet tree

Pests and diseases: The various *Tabebuia* species are susceptible to red spider mite damage. These pests should be treated by a licensed exterminator.

Uses: Industrially, *Tabebuia* trees are best known for the quality of their wood. These trees produce extremely durable, salt tolerant, light- to medium-weight timber. This wood is used commercially in the production of furniture, paneling, cabinets, wooden bowls, and floorboards. Traditionally, the Carib people have used *Tabebuia* wood for canoe building, and the trees are sometimes planted as shade for coffee and cocoa crops.

Trees in the *Tabebuia* genus have medicinal uses as well. A concentrate made from boiling the flowers, leaves, and roots of this plant can be used to reduce fevers and pain, to induce sweating, and to treat tonsil inflammation. Decoctions made from the cortex of the tree are prescribed to treat a wide variety of ailments, from anemia and constipation to malaria and uterine cancer. This drink is also consumed to eliminate intestinal parasites.

Above
Tabebuia rosea
Rosy trumpet tree flower, leaves and fruits at various stages of growth

Tamarix aphylla
Athel Tree, Athel Pine

Tamarix is a genus of 54 species of deciduous shrubs and small trees. Commonly known as tamarisks, these hardy, vigorous, conifer-like plants are native to the Mediterranean, India, the Arabian Peninsula, East Asia, and North, East and Central Africa.

***Tamarix aphylla*, athel tree, athel pine:** An evergreen, upright, medium-size tree, the athel pine is fast-growing, quickly reaching its mature height of 10–18m. Immature trees have light grey trunks and stems, while mature trees have a trunk measuring up to 1m in diameter, covered in thick, rough, dark grey to black bark, from which emerge grey-brown stems. The trees have a strong, woody root system which penetrates deeply throughout the soil, about 10m vertically, and spreads wide, up to 34m horizontally.

Tamarix aphylla trees have a rounded or irregular, spreading crown, which reaches a diameter of up to 6m. The crown is composed of many heavy, stout branches and long, pendulous, jointed, wiry and very slender twigs. Athel trees have attractive, feathery foliage consisting of alternate, small, scale- or needle-like, greyish-green leaves, arranged along the branches. The leaves secrete salt, which forms a crusty layer on their surface, and also drips on the ground beneath the tree.

Blooming in spring and summer, the athel pine produces large numbers of small, pale pink or whitish colored flowers. These stalkless blossoms appear at the end of branches, borne in elongated racemes or spikes measuring 3–6cm long. *Tamarix aphylla* is a monoecious species, with separate male and female flowers emerging on the same tree. Each tiny flower has five sepals and five petals, with each petal measuring only 2mm long. Male flowers have five stamens. Female flowers are followed by bell-shaped, capsule-like fruits, containing many small cylindrical seeds. The seeds have a tuft of fine hairs which assists wind dispersal, for natural regeneration.

Opposite page
Tamarix aphylla
Athel tree flowers

Opposite page
Tamarix aphylla
Athel tree leaves
and manicured tree

Care: *Tamarix aphylla* trees flourish in dry locations, sandy soil, and full sun, making them perfect additions to Gulf gardens. They are highly resistant to saline and alkaline soils, drought tolerant, and able to withstand strong winds, making them excellent choices for desert landscapes. During the growing season they require ample water and monthly applications of a balanced liquid fertilizer. Athel pines need little maintenance; plant in well-drained soil, cut back young trees almost to ground level after planting, and prune yearly once trees are established.

Propagation: From seed, cuttings, or by suckering. To propagate from seed, sow seeds as soon as they are ripe in potting containers. When using cuttings, root hardwood cuttings in winter or semi-ripe cuttings in summer.

Pests and diseases: Plants in the *Tamarix* genus are not commonly susceptible to pests and diseases.

Uses: Products and by-products of the athel pine are used for a variety of industrial, medicinal, and landscaping purposes. *Tamarix aphylla* wood is used for fuel, and produces a fragrant scent when burned. The wood is fine grained, light colored, and capable of taking a high polish, which makes it appropriate for use in the production of furniture, fences, and posts. The bark of the tree is a rich source of tannin and mordant for dyeing. Athel tree flowers provide an important source of pollen for the honeybee, and galls, or growths, on the flowers are used for tanning leather.

Medicinally, the bark of the tree can be boiled, and vinegar added to the liquid, to make a rinse for the treatment of lice. The bark is also used in treating eczema and other skin ailments. Athel pine branches can be boiled, and the resulting sugary liquid used to treat fever, as well as snake and scorpion bites. Ash from the burned wood has been known to relieve hemorrhoids. The leaves of this tree, when boiled and mixed with ginger, have been used to treat issues with the uterus. Fresh, green leaves can be crushed and made into a poultice, which can be applied to the head to treat sunstroke. An application of fresh leaves to skin in the early morning is also said to treat vitiligo. Apply a poultice of crushed leaves to affected areas for 10–15 minutes at a time, for three days. Decoctions made from flower galls are used as an astringent and gargle, and the fruits are said to stimulate appetite.

Although considered a weed in Australia, *Tamarix aphylla* is planted for landscaping purposes in the Middle East to form windbreaks, privacy screens and as a source of shade. This tree is also highly valued as an agent for erosion control throughout arid and semi-arid regions. It is known for stabilizing sand dunes due to its fast growth, deep and extensive root system, and ability to resist burial by shifting sand.

Opposite page
Tamarix aphylla
Athel tree

Tecoma stans
Yellow Bells

Tecoma is a small genus of about 12 distinct species of evergreen climbers, scrambling shrubs, and upright trees. Native to South and Central America, the southern United States, and Africa, plants in this genus feature foliage composed of pinnate, or sometimes tri-foliate, opposite leaves, with ovate-oblong to rounded leaflets. This group of plants produces flowers that are narrowly bell- to funnel- shaped, five-lobed, and yellow, orange, or red depending on the species. Blooms emerge in dense, terminal racemes or panicles.

Tecoma stans, yellow bells: The yellow bell is an open, ascending or upright plant that can be grown as a shrub or small tree. It often has several slim trunks if grown as a tree, and makes an attractive multi-trunk tree. Reaching a mature height of 5–9m and spreading to a width of 3–5m, this plant has foliage consisting of pinnate leaves, each about 35cm long, composed of five to 13 oblong-ovate to lance-shaped, saw-tooth edged, bright green leaflets. This tree takes its common name, yellow bells, from its clusters of bright yellow bell-shaped flowers. These blossoms, measuring 5cm in length, emerge in terminal racemes up to 15cm long. Yellow bells flower twice a year, in early spring and autumn, and the blooms are followed by fruits in the form of long, slender, capsule-shaped seedpods.

Yellow bells are highly decorative plants. Due to their tolerance of the harsh Gulf climate, they are considered one of the most famous ornamental trees in the region. *Tecoma stans* can be found throughout the Arabian Gulf in public and private gardens, roadsides, and parks. These plants are versatile additions to any landscape; they are beautiful when grown in rows, or as a focus point in the garden as a specimen tree.

Care: *Tecoma* plants flourish in dry locations, sandy soil, and full sun or partial shade, making them perfect additions to Gulf gardens. During the growing season they require ample water and monthly applications of a balanced liquid fertilizer. Yellow bells require regular pruning to maintain a balanced shape. The optimum time to prune *Tecoma stans* is after flowering.

Propagation: From seed or cuttings.

Pests and diseases: Plants in the *Tecoma* genus are susceptible to red spider mite and whitefly damage. Both of these pests should be treated by a licensed exterminator.

Opposite page
Tecoma stans
Yellow bells flowers

Above
Tecoma stans
Yellow bells

Left
Tecoma stans
Yellow bells flowers, fruit, leaves and trunk

Tecomella undulata
Desert Teak

Native to India, Pakistan, Iran and extending into the Arabian Peninsula, *Tecomella* is a genus of approximately 25 distinct species of evergreen or deciduous shrubs and trees.

Tecomella undulata (synonym *Tecoma undulata*), desert teak: A slow-growing, upright, deciduous or semi-evergreen tree, the desert teak reaches a mature height of 10m and spreads to a width of 10m. Its trunk, measuring 40cm in diameter and greyish or yellowish brown in color, supports a spreading crown and drooping branches. The bark of this tree is soft and greenish-brown when the plant is young, turning hard and dark brown as the tree ages.

Tecomella undulata features foliage consisting of alternate, simple, narrow, somewhat lance-shaped leaves. These leaves are entire, with wavy margins, and are rounded at the tips. They measure 5–12cm in length. This foliage serves as a backdrop for the tree's large, eye-catching yellow, orange and red flowers. The desert teak blooms in spring, producing dense, terminal clusters or racemes of up to seven blossoms. Each flower has a funnel-shaped corolla, and averages between 6.5 and 7.5cm in length. The blooms are followed by elongated, flattened

Opposite page
Tecomella undulata
Desert teak flowers

Above
Tecomella undulata
Desert teak

Right
Tecomella undulata
Desert teak

and slightly curved capsule-shaped fruits. The capsules are 15–20cm long, and contain winged seeds.

Care: *Tecomella undulata* trees are a viable choice for Gulf gardens, as they thrive in full sun and are tolerant of dry conditions. However, these plants do need regular watering, well-drained soil, and monthly fertilization with a liquid fertilizer during the growing season. Desert teak trees should be pruned once a year.

Propagation: From seed or cuttings.

Pests and diseases: Plants in the *Tecomella* genus are susceptible to red spider mite damage. These pests should be treated by a licensed exterminator.

Uses: *Tecomella undulata* is an important part of the landscape in arid regions. It can grow on stabilized sand dunes and acts as a windbreak. The rooting system of the tree is extensive, forming a wide network under the soil's surface, an attribute that makes it a valuable species in the battle against soil erosion. The shade of tree's crown provides shelter for birds, desert wildlife, and animal herds, and its leaves, flowers, and fruit pods are fodder for camels, goats, and sheep. In cities it is commonly planted as a street tree.

Products from the desert teak serve a variety of uses. Its wood is strong, tough, and durable, and is excellent for firewood and charcoal. Traditionally, *Tecomella undulata* is considered one of the most important medicinal plants of Rajasthan, India. The bark of the tree is used as a remedy for syphilis, urinary disorders, liver diseases, gonorrhea, and enlargement of the spleen, and to treat skin ailments such as leucoderma. Desert teak flowers are an ingredient in hepatitis treatments, and the seeds, crushed with pinus leaf extract, make a poultice to soothe hemorrhoids and treat abscesses.

Above
Tecomella undulata
Desert teak fruits, leaves and flowers

Thespesia populnea
Umbrella Tree, Indian Tulip Tree, Aden Apple

Native to the coastal areas of the Indian and Pacific Oceans, from East Africa and India to mainland Southeast Asia, Indonesia, and the Philippines, as well as subtropical regions throughout the world, *Thespesia* is a genus of more than 17 species of evergreen, perennial shrubs and trees.

***Thespesia populnea* (synonym *Hibiscus populneus*), umbrella tree, Indian tulip tree, aden apple:** Successfully grown throughout the Arabian Gulf as an ornamental tree, *Thespesia populnea* is a small or medium-sized, fast-growing, evergreen, flowering tree. Known by the common names umbrella tree, Indian tulip tree, and aden apple, this erect to spreading plant reaches a mature height of 6–20m and spreads to a width of 5–8m. With a trunk measuring 20–30cm in diameter, aden apples are bushy, carrying a dense crown supported by a trunk covered in brown or pale grey bark. The trunk sprouts corrugated, scaly twigs and becomes rugged with deep fissures as the tree ages. These trees feature foliage composed of alternate, simple, heart-shaped to ovate leaves borne on long stalks, or petioles, measuring 5–10cm in length. Each shiny, light to dark green leaf measures from 6–12cm, tapering at the tip, with nectar-bearing zones at the bases of the midribs. *Thespesia populnea* is sometimes confused with another closely related species genus, *Hibiscus tiliaceus*; the two plants can, however, be distinguished by their leaf forms. The leaves of *Hibiscus tiliaceus* are wider, with dense star-shaped hairs on their lower surfaces.

Thespesia populnea trees are flower bearing, producing solitary, short-lived, cup-shaped, pale yellow or yellowish-orange blossoms emerging from the leaf axils. These blooms resemble those of *Hibiscus tiliaceus*, although they lack red stigma. Each flower has five spreading petals, 5–8cm across, with a maroon or purple center. Although the flowers of this tree are short-lived, turning maroon or dull purple and dropping one to two days after opening, the tree maintains its splendor by blooming in sequence throughout the year in warm areas.

Thespesia populnea trees are usually pollinated by birds, and produce fruit in the form of apple-shaped, flattened, leathery fruit capsules. These fruits, spherical in shape with disc-like sepals, are initially green, ripening from brown to black, and contain a bright yellow gum. The fruit dries as it matures, eventually opening to release five to eight greyish brown or black seeds. The seeds are covered with dense, short hairs. Both the pod and the seeds are buoyant and can travel long distances in the sea.

Care: *Thespesia populnea* thrives in sunny locations in sandy coastal soils, but also grows in volcanic, limestone, and rocky soils. Soil should be enriched monthly with a balanced liquid fertilizer during the growing season. This species' ability to thrive in sandy, saline soils make it useful when planted as coastal windbreaks. It resists salt spray, wind action, and brackish water. Trees in the *Thespesia* genus require daily watering, particularly during the summer months. Regular pruning is necessary for the tree to maintain a balanced shape.

Opposite page
Thespesia populnea
Umbrella tree flower

Right
Thespesia populnea
Umbrella tree

Propagation: *Thespesia populnea* trees can be propagated from seed, rooting cuttings, or by air laying in spring time. Seed pods are indehiscent, which means the pods do not open when mature. To propagate by seed, the capsules must be opened by hand and the seeds removed. Scar the seeds using an emery board, sand paper or nail clippers, taking care not to reach the tender embryo inside the seed. Soak scarred seeds in warm, fresh water for at least 24 hours before planting. Plant seeds in moist, sandy soil; germination usually takes place in 14–28 days. To propagate using cuttings, cut a length of branch about 30cm long, treat with rooting hormone, and plant.

Pests and diseases: *Thespesia populnea* trees are susceptible to whitefly and red spider mite damage. These should both be treated by a licensed exterminator.

Uses: All parts of the *Thespesia populnea* tree are used for a wide variety of purposes. Rope can be made from the tough, fibrous outer bark, and the inner bark is used for making finer cordage. The bark also yields oil tannin used for tanning leather, and gum in the form of a dark red resin. The wood of this tree produces a yellow dye used to dye wool. *Thespesia populnea* trees produce a hard, termite-resistant timber known as Pacific rosewood. This wood is naturally oily, so it can be highly polished, and does not impart a flavor, so it is often used to carve wooden food bowls. It is also used to make musical instruments. The fruits, flowers, and young leaves of the tree are edible raw or cooked. Aden apple seeds contain water, raw protein, and fixed oil. Lamp oil can be made from this seed oil. Seed capsules also yield a yellowish-green color.

Medicinally, the ground-up bark of the *Thespesia populnea* tree is used to treat skin diseases, dysentery and hemorrhoids. The leaves of the tree can be made into a poultice and applied to inflamed and swollen joints. The yellowish juice extracted from young fruits is used to treat insect bites, gonorrhea, ringworm, and migraine headache, and is also used for fistula, psoriasis, scabies, sprains, and wart removal. Topically, the seeds of *Thespesia populnea* can be applied to treat scabies and other skin diseases, and are rubbed on swollen joints.

Agriculturally, *Thespesia populnea* is planted on coffee and tea plantations in India, to provide shade for crops. For landscaping purposes, this species is often cultivated as a specimen plant, grown in small gardens or in pots for placement on patios. It is planted in public areas as a street tree or small shade tree, and is frequently seen in coastal regions, where the trees serve as a natural windbreak for strong sea winds.

Above
Thespesia populnea
Umbrella tree fruits, flowers and leaves

Vitex agnus-castus
Chaste Tree

Native to tropical and subtropical regions throughout the world, *Vitex* is a widespread genus of 250 species of deciduous or evergreen trees and shrubs. Plants in this genus feature foliage consisting of opposite, entire to palmately compound leaves, and produce flowers in terminal panicles, racemes, or cymes. These blossoms are tubular, two-lipped, and purple or white in color.

Vitex agnus-castus, chaste tree: *Vitex agnus-castus*, commonly known as the chaste tree, is an open, spreading, semi-deciduous small tree or shrub. Native to the Mediterranean region, this plant reaches a maximum height and width of 2–8m. Chaste trees have attractive, aromatic foliage consisting of five-foliate palmately compound leaves composed of slender, narrowly elliptic or lance-shaped, dark green leaflets. These pointed leaflets measure 10–15cm long, and are slightly toothed on the edges. Chaste tree foliage is green on the top and several shades paler on the underside, giving the tree an overall grey-green appearance.

Vitex agnus-castus produces slender, upright, terminal panicles of small, spiky, tubular flowers. These fragrant blossoms come in shades of purple to dark blue and are sometimes white on the ends. The chaste tree has its first flowering of the season in autumn, when the plant turns almost mauve in color.

Vitex agnus-castus is a fast-growing plant, and it must be pruned in early spring if it is to be maintained as a shrub. The chaste tree thrives in full sun or partial shade, and can be planted in a group as a colorful natural privacy screen, or alone as the focal point of the garden.

Care: *Vitex* trees should be planted in a location receiving full sunlight. They do well in sandy soil, and are drought tolerant. These trees are easy to maintain, and only require pruning once a year.

Propagation: By seed. *Vitex* species may also be propagated in summer using semi-ripe cuttings.

Pests and diseases: Members of the *Vitex* genus are not commonly susceptible to pests or diseases.

Uses: Many parts of the *Vitex trifolia* tree are useful for a variety of purposes. The soft wood of this tree is used in basket weaving, and the leaves of the tree can be dried and burned as a natural insect repellent. Medicinally, the leaves can also be used to reduce fever. The most valuable part of the Arabian lilac tree, however, is its oil-producing fruit. Oil from the fruit of *Vitex trifolia* has a wide variety of medicinal properties. It is a natural libido inhibitor, and as such has been consumed for centuries by priests and prisoners for this purpose. *Vitex trifolia* oil has the ability to regulate women's menstrual cycles, and can reduce the effects of Pre-Menstrual Syndrome (PMS). It has been given in the treatment of migraines, and can be applied externally to relieve joint pain. Arabian lilac oil may be purchased commercially from pharmacies in capsule form, or the small fruit can be soaked in hot water to make tea.

Opposite page
Vitex sp.
Chaste tree flowers

Right
Vitex sp.
Chaste tree

Above
Vitex sp.
Chaste tree fruits, flowers and leaves

Palms

Left
Phoenix dactylifera
Date palm flowers

Introduction to palms

Native to tropical and subtropical regions such as Africa, Southern Asia, the Pacific Islands, the Americas, and even as far north as the Northern Mediterranean, palm is the common name given to a vast group of plants that thrive in warm climates. There are more than 2,700 different species of palms, and they vary widely in size, foliage, flowers, and fruit. Palms are vital to many populations around the world; they provide both food and industrial materials, and are second only to grasses in their importance. In addition, palms are beautiful, diverse plants, and are a staple of landscaping in warmer regions.

The trunks of most palm trees are tall and upright, although some species have trunks that lie on the ground, and others that are mostly buried under the soil. They may have smooth or rough bark, and some even have thorns. The average girth of a palm trunk is 50cm, although some palms have trunks that are up to 1.5m in diameter. The height of palm trees ranges from just a few centimeters to over 30m tall.

The leaves, or fronds, of the various palm species vary greatly in both size and appearance. The smallest palms have fronds that are less than 30cm long. Palms can actually be divided into two distinct groups based on the shape of their fronds and midribs. Palm leaves are either:

Palmate: Palmate leaves are fan-like. They range from 60–120cm in width and are generally hand-shaped. An example of a palm with palmate fronds is *Washingtonia filifera*.

Pinnate: Pinnate leaves are feather-like. This type of frond grows up to 6m long and ranges from 30–120cm in width. An example of a palm with pinnate fronds is *Phoenix dactylifera* (date palm).

Palm types may also be classified based on the kind of spines that grow off the stalk of the frond. There are three major spine categories. Some palms have strong, arched spines, like *Washingtonia filifera*. A second type of palm has pointed, sharp, thorn-like spines. The last group of palms have fronds with spineless stalks.

Propagation: Palm tree fruits vary greatly in size and shape depending on the species, and the success of a tree's fruit depends on fertilization. Many palm tree species are such that the male and female flowers are on different trees. Palms depend on wind or insects for pollination.

There are three main modes of propagation for palm trees:

From seed: Most palm species are grown from seed. Sow fresh seeds singly, as soon as the fruits are ripe, in standard compost. Place each seed in a container 6–7cm in diameter. Cover the seed with its own depth in compost. Germination times vary widely among palm species: the seeds of most species sprout within two to three months, although some germinate as quickly as 10 days and others take up to two years.

Opposite page
Sabal palmetto
Cabbage palm

Above
Palmate leaves

By sucker: Suckers are derived from the base of the main plant. These suckers can be removed from the "mother" tree and transplanted to a new location. To propagate a new tree using a sucker, it must be prepared before separation. First, remove the leaves around the base of the sucker, and cut the remaining leaves down to a third of the diameter of the overall plant. Next, cover the plant with hessian for a few months. Then, remove the sucker plant from the parent tree. This removal process should only be done in spring or autumn. When separating the plants, be sure that the sucker is removed with its leaves and roots. To replant the sucker, dig a hole deeper than the level the sucker was growing on the main plant. Place the sucker in the hole, then fill it with natural fertilizer and compost. Finally, place stones around the base of the plant to reduce water evaporation.

From cellular tissue: The technology now exists to propagate palm trees using cellular tissue. This process of propogation can only be done in laboratories.

Separating mature trees: Palm trees can be propagated by separating and transplanting mature trees. This process is the same as removing a sucker. Often this is done in nurseries, where gardeners may purchase mature trees. When transplanting a mature, store bought tree into a garden, find a location where the tree is separate, both from other palms and from other types of plants. If more than one of the same kind of palm is purchased, similar types of palms should be planted in proximity to each other, in clusters of three to five. However, there should be at least 5m between each tree. To prepare the

land, dig a hole 1–2m deep by 1m wide (depending on the size of the palm). Place a mixture of equal parts sand, mud, and fertilizer in the hole. Leave this mixture in the ground for three months before planting the tree; this is so the natural fertilizer will sink into and enrich the surrounding soil. After three months have passed, place the tree in the hole, packing the soil tight around the base of the palm. This helps to hold the roots of the tree. Place supports on the trunk if necessary, remove the outer leaves from the trunk, and wrap the top fronds in burlap. This burlap may be removed as soon as new growth appears.

Uses: The palm tree's attractive shape makes it a favorite choice of landscapers. These trees are used to decorate public gardens, streets, sea shores, and riversides around the world. Palms are not just decorative, however; they have been a source of food, clothing, building materials and fuel for centuries. Palm fibers are used for making ropes and brooms, and for caulking ships. The tips of palm fronds are woven into mats, hats, and baskets. The sugary sap from palms, such as the Palmyra, can be made into food and sweet drinks, and starch from palms, such as the sago, are used in food. Many familiar palm fruits are edible, such as dates and coconuts, and these fruits are often dried and used in cakes and other sweets. Oil from palm fruits is very versatile, and is used for lighting, in foods such as salad oils, cooking fats, and margarine, and in soaps and hair products. Even the seeds of palm fruits are valuable, and often made into buttons and other carvings.

Above
Pinnate leaves

Acoelorrhaphe wrightii
Saw Palm, Everglades Palm

Native to Florida, Mexico, Central America, and the West Indies, *Acoelorrhaphe* is a genus of only one distinct species of palm.

***Acoelorrhaphe wrightii*, saw palm, Everglades palm:** The saw palm is a small to moderately tall tree, reaching a maximum height of 5–10m, and spreading to a width of 2.5–6m. Each saw palm has between three and 10 slender, upright trunks, forming tight clumps. The trunks are covered with brown fibers and old leaf bases. Sprouting from the top of each trunk are rounded, deeply cut, palmate leaves with spiny stalks. These fronds are a glossy mid-green color on the top and light, silvery-green underneath. The fronds grow as long as 1m, and the sections of each leaf are joined together for half their length. Saw palms bloom in summer, producing small, bowl-shaped, hermaphroditic white flowers. These blossoms emerge in slender panicles, growing up to 1m in length, and are hidden behind leaves. The flowers are followed by black fruit. This tree makes a striking addition to any landscape.

Saw palms grow into steadily larger and thicker clumps if left untended. Remove suckers to prevent the formation of additional trunks, and prune stems to give the palm an open, attractive appearance.

Care: *Acoelorrhaphe* palms are resilient trees that can handle the harsh Arabian Gulf climate. They thrive when planted in direct sunlight, and are not adversely affected by high temperatures, strong winds, or saline-rich sands. To truly flourish, saw palms require moist, well-drained soil, enhanced with a monthly application of a balanced liquid fertilizer. They do best in humid conditions, and need generous watering throughout the growing season.

Propagation: From seed. Seeds must be soaked for two to three days in warm water before planting; change the water every 24 hours during this period to prevent rotting. After sowing, seeds will germinate within two to three months. *Acoelorrhaphe wrightii* can also be propagated by dividing clumps of existing trees.

Pests and diseases: Saw palms are susceptible to red spider mite damage. These pests should be treated by a licensed exterminator.

Opposite page
Acoelorrhaphe wrightii
Saw palms

Right
Acoelorrhaphe wrightii
Saw palms

Above

Acoelorrhaphe wrightii
Saw palm trunk
and fruits

Bismarckia nobilis
Silver Frond Palm

Native only to the western and northern regions of the island of Madagascar, *Bismarckia* is a genus of only one species of palm tree.

***Bismarckia nobilis*, silver frond palm:** The silver frond palm is a gray to tan or brown, single-stemmed tree. This palm varies widely in size, ranging from 2–24m in height, with a trunk ranging from 30–45cm in diameter. The trunk bulges slightly at the bottom, and is covered in fine, woolly hairs. It is smooth and largely free of leaf bases, except in areas of newer growth. The full leaf crown of this plant is 7m tall and 6m wide, rounded to oblong in shape, and composed of large, palmate leaves. The foliage of this tree is a striking silver-blue, although there are green-leaved varieties (which are less cold-tolerant). Silver frond palms have almost round leaves that can grow over 3m wide. Each leaf is divided to a third of its length into 20 or more stiff, once-folded segments, themselves split on the ends. The leaves are costa-palmate and induplicate, which means the "v" in the accordion folds of the frond opens towards the sky. The hastula, or section where the blade and petioles meet, is wedge-shaped. The petioles of the silver frond palm are 2–3m in length, slightly armed, and have a few short spines along their margins. They are covered in a white wax and cinnamon-colored caducous scales.

Bismarckia nobilis is a dioecious species, meaning there are separate male and female trees. These trees produce pendent, interfoliar inflorescences of small brown flowers. In female plants this flower is followed by brown, ovoid fruits, each containing a single seed.

With their large, dramatic leaves, silver frond palms are best planted where they can serve as a focal point in the garden. Their silver-blue hue provides a striking contrast to the typical dark green background of the average landscape.

Care: *Bismarckia* palms are hardy plants that flourish in direct sunlight. They are able to survive high temperatures, up to 50°C, and can also tolerate strong winds, as well as ground with a high saline content. Silver frond palms need to be planted in fertile, moist, well-drained, humus-rich soil, and do best in humid conditions. These plants need ample water and fertilizer to grow and thrive.

Propagation: From seed. Seeds typically germinate within six to eight weeks.

Pests and diseases: Silver frond palms are susceptible to scale insect damage. These pests should be treated by a licensed exterminator.

Uses: The trunk of the silver frond palm is used in construction. It can be cut into planks or used to build wall partitions. In ancient times, the soft, woolly hairs covering the trunk were prized as a material for upholstery stuffing. They were used in only the finest furniture, as stuffing for the king's throne and for chairs in the king's court. These fibers are still considered valuable and are highly sought-after by craftsmen. The leaves of *Bismarckia nobilis* are used in roof thatching. These fronds can also be woven into baskets. The pith of the fruit of this tree is edible, and is considered a slightly bitter sago.

Opposite page
Bismarckia nobilis
Silver frond palms

Right
Bismarckia nobilis
Silver frond palm fruits

Left
Bismarckia nobilis
Silver frond palm flowers

Caryota mitis
Burmese Fishtail Palm

Native to Burma, the Malaysian Peninsula, Indonesia and the Philippines, the genus *Caryota* is composed of only 12–13 species of single- and cluster-stemmed, monoecious, sometimes monocarpic, palms. *Caryota* palms are easily recognizable by their unique leaf arrangement. This is the only palm genus with bi-pinnate leaves; each frond has a prominent sheathing base, and leaves are arranged in spirals on the upper part of each stem.

Palms in the *Caryota* genus take their common name, fishtail palm, from their unusual, wedge-shaped, jagged-ended leaflets. The fronds have elongated leaf crowns, in which the leaves grow not only from the top of the trunk but also down its length. As the palm blooms, inflorescences form at each leaf node, from the top down. The palm produces both male and female blossoms, almost in separate inflorescences. After flowering, the trunks die off and the fruits mature. Any gaps formed by spent trunks are filled by new growth in clumping palms.

Caryota mitis, **Burmese fishtail palm:** This small to medium-sized evergreen ornamental has clustered, densely packed stems, at first clothed with fibrous leaf bases, and later bare. Commonly known as the Burmese fishtail palm, *Caryota mitis* grows to a maximum height of 3–12m, spreads to a width of 3–7m, and has trunks measuring approximately 15cm in diameter. Its slender trunks are topped with several broadly linear, bi-pinnate, light green leaves, each 2–4m long. These fronds are composed of between six and 60, fishtail-like, asymmetrically three-angled leaflets, measuring 15cm in length.

The Burmese fishtail palm has an unusual flowering pattern. Each trunk produces flowers for several seasons. The tiny purplish or cream, three-petalled, cup-shaped flowers, each only 2cm across, are borne in inflorescences that are nestled amongst or below the tree's leaves. Emerging in summer, each inflorescence can range from 30cm to 1.5m long, with up to 60 flowering branches or pendent panicles. The flowers appear in threes, one female flower in between two male ones. The flowers bloom in a kind of cascading pattern; the first flowering mop-like cluster emerges from the top of the mature palm, subsequent clusters emerge below, and so on. When the cluster reaches the ground, the palm dies.

Caryota mitis produces rounded, dark purple or red fruits, measuring approximately 13mm in diameter.

Caution: **The fruit of the Burmese fishtail palm contains oxalic acid, which is toxic when ingested, and may also cause severe chemical burns to the skin. Although the fruits hang high off the ground, since they only emerge once the tree is mature, it is best to remove and discard fruit bunches as they begin to ripen, particularly if children are present.**

Opposite page
Caryota mitis
Burmese fishtail palms

Care: *Caryota* palms are resilient trees that can survive easily in the harsh Arabian Gulf climate. They thrive when planted in direct sunlight or partial shade, and are not adversely affected by high temperatures or strong summer winds. To truly flourish, these plants require moist, well-drained soil, enhanced with fertilizer. During the growing season, fishtail palms need moderate watering and a monthly application of a balanced liquid fertilizer.

Propagation: From seed, root division, or from the numerous suckers growing from the base of the plant. Seeds can be stored until use by removing their fleshy coating. Propagate by seed in spring; wear gloves to protect the hands when planting seeds. Seed germination occurs within three to four months.

Pests and diseases: *Caryota* palms are susceptible to red spider mite and scale insect damage. These pests should be treated by a licensed exterminator.

Uses: In India, the fishtail palm is used for a variety of purposes. Fuzz from the young leaves is used as tinder for fires. The palm is used in construction; the leaves serve as roof thatching, and fibers from the leaf sheath are made into rope. The fronds can be woven into household items, and the seeds are made into decorative beads. For cooking purposes, an edible starch (sago) is extracted from the stem, and the heart of the palm is eaten. Like other palms it is also tapped for sap, which is made into palm sugar or fermented to make toddy. Medicinally, leaf fibers are used to treat poisonous animal bites and insect stings.

The fishtail palm is an attractive plant, and can serve a variety of landscaping purposes. Young specimens may be used as houseplants, or they may be planted in the garden singly as ornamental specimens or in a group for a screen that has a coarse, ferny texture.

Opposite page and above
Caryota mitis Burmese fishtail palm fruits at various stages of growth and leaves

Chamaerops humilis
Dwarf Fan Palm

Native to Europe and the Mediterranean region, the genus *Chamaerops* is composed of only one distinct species of shrubby, clumping palm.

***Chamaerops humilis*, dwarf fan palm:** The dwarf fan palm features several slow-growing stems that emerge from a single base. These trunks, often clumped tightly together, grow to an average height of between 60cm and 3m, and have an average girth of 20–25cm. This tree spreads to an overall width of 1–2m, and is suitable for coastal gardens as a specimen plant.

Dwarf fan palms have light green to bluish or greyish foliage. Their fan-shaped fronds, measuring 60cm in diameter, are deeply-lobed, with long petioles terminating in a spray of 12–15 linear leaflets. Each leaflet grows 60–100cm long, forming accordion-like folds one-third to two-thirds of the way from the base. This top portion of the leaf is narrow, tough, and stiff to the touch. Needle-like spines protrude from the leaf stem, protecting the plant from animals.

Chamaerops humilis blooms in spring and summer, producing tiny, yellow, three-petalled flowers, emerging in dense panicles which are about 35cm long. These mostly hidden blossoms grow from the lower leaf axils. Dwarf fan palms are dioecious, with male and female flowers on separate plants. These flowers are followed by fruits that are bright green when new, maturing to a dull yellow and ripening to brown in the fall months (September–November).

Care: *Chamaerops* palms require moist, well-drained soil, enhanced with a monthly application of a balanced liquid fertilizer. They thrive when planted in direct sunlight or partial shade, and need only moderate watering during the growing season. Dwarf fan palms are resilient plants, appropriate for Arabian Gulf gardens due to their tolerance for high temperatures, summer winds, and ground with a high saline content.

Propagation: From seed. *Chamaerops humilis* also produces suckers when mature, and these suckers can be separated from established plants in late spring.

Pests and diseases: Dwarf fan palms are susceptible to red spider mite damage, which should be treated by a licensed exterminator.

Uses: The leaves of the adult dwarf fan palm have been used in weaving baskets and mats, and in making brooms. The fruits of this plant are inedible as food, although they are used in traditional medicine.

Opposite page
Chamaerops humilis
Dwarf fan palms

Above
Chamaerops humilis
Dwarf fan palm fruits

Copernicia alba
Caranday Palm, Wax Palm

The genus *Copernicia* is composed of approximately 24 species of slow-growing, single-stemmed palms. Native to Cuba, Argentina and Brazil, trees in this genus range from 5–30m in height, and have a maximum spread of up to 4.5m.

***Copernicia alba*, caranday palm, wax palm:** The wax palm, a native of South America, is a slow growing tree with a very hard, single, grey, cylindrical-shaped trunk. This trunk, about 30cm in diameter when mature, supports a circular crown. The trunk retains spiny old leaf bases when the tree is young, which fall off as the plant ages. *Copernicia alba* can range from 6–30m full-grown, and spreads to a width of 4.5m.

The wax palm features foliage composed of palmate, or fan shaped, leaves which grow from the top of the trunk, borne in dense, terminal clusters. The fronds are round, 75–80cm in diameter, with 30–35 segments. Each segment is induplicate, or folded inward, slightly forked, 35cm long and 4–5cm wide. *Copernicia alba* leaves are glaucous, and range in color from greyish-green to pure green above, and are silvery green beneath. Adult leaves are covered on both sides with small red points or dots. They rest on petioles that are 1.2–1.3m long including the leaf sheath, with very sharp spines on each side. Faded leaves remain on the trunk, hanging down to form a thatch-like skirt.

Caranday palms bloom in fall, producing small, solitary or grouped, bowl-shaped, white or pale cream flowers. These tiny blossoms are hermaphroditic, three-petalled with three sepals, and measure only 10–20mm in width. Flowers are borne in panicles between the leaves. In summer, *Copernicia alba* produces edible, berry-like fruits. Fruits are round, with a single oval seed inside, initially yellow in color and turning dark green or black as they ripen. These fruits are juicy and have a sweet taste, although they leave an astringent aftertaste in the mouth.

Care: *Copernicia* palms are resilient trees that can survive the harsh Arabian Gulf climate. They thrive when planted in direct sunlight or partial shade, and are not adversely affected by high temperatures or strong summer winds. To truly flourish, these plants require moist, well-drained soil, enhanced with fertilizer. During the growing season, water tree freely and apply a balanced liquid fertilizer monthly. *Copernicia* palms are most successful when planted in an area with humid conditions.

Propagation: By separating suckers from mature plants, or by seed in spring. Seeds typically germinate 30–45 days if the fruit is ripe when harvested. Germination can be accelerated by removing the exocarp and mesocarp (outer and middle layers) of the fruit, cleaning the seed, and soaking it in water at normal temperature for five to seven days. Seeds should be sown into peat moss or sand, in seedbeds that are at least 10cm deep.

Pests and diseases: Palms in the *Copernicia* genus are susceptible to red spider mite damage. The larvae of this insect infect and attack the endosperm of the seed. These pests should be treated by a licensed exterminator.

Opposite page
Copernicia alba
Wax palm

Right
Copernicia alba
Wax palms

Uses: Commercially, *Copernicia alba* is perhaps best known for the wax it produces. This wax is used in the manufacturing of lipstick, candles, and some car polishes. However, all parts of the tree are useful. The trunk is very hard and is used for telephone poles. Timber from the trunk is also used to make posts, and in building construction for fences, walls, and floors. In Argentina, *Copernicia alba* trunks are made into plant pots for both the domestic market and for export to Europe. The leaves are woven into baskets, hats, lampshades and hand-fans, and old inflorescences are used as brooms. Due to its long flowering period, honey producers place hives among the palms to obtain high quality single-flower honey. The roots can be boiled, and this decoction is used by doctors and veterinarians in the treatment of musculoskeletal, blood and cardiovascular ailments.

For landscaping purposes, larger varieties of the *Copernicia* palm are suitable for lawn specimens or in courtyards, while smaller species make attractive container plants. *Copernicia alba* can be planted singly or in groups, and are widely used in public spaces such as parks, shopping avenues, and roundabouts, as well as in private flower beds and gardens.

Above
Copernicia alba
Wax palm flowers

Dypsis decaryi
Triangle Palm, Three-sided Palm

Native to the island of Madagascar, the genus *Dypsis* is composed of more than 150 species of solitary-trunked or clustering palms. Ranging in size from tiny to towering, almost all *Dypsis* species have a crownshaft, and many have plumose leaves, while there are some palmate varieties. This monoecious tree bears unisex flowers, meaning that separate male and female flowers grow on the same plant. Inflorescences are formed mostly from within the leaf crown, although sometimes they are situated beneath it. Palms in the *Dypsis* genus produce fruits that are usually brightly colored, although in some species they are black or brown.

***Dypsis decaryi* (synonym *Neodypsis decaryi*), triangle palm, three-sided palm:** A slow to moderate growing palm, *Dypsis decaryi* grows to an eventual height ranging from 8–15m. This tree has a solitary trunk, approximately 50cm in diameter, covered in brownish-grey bark and ringed with scars from spent fronds. The tree's stocky trunk supports a leaf crown that is 4.5m wide and tall. This plant takes its common name, triangle palm, from the three distinct sets of overlapping leaf-bases that emerge in a triangular pattern from the trunk. As leaves fade they fall from the trunk, giving a distinctive inverted triangle shape to the leaf crown.

The triangle palm has foliage consisting of pinnate, or feather-like, leaves. Arching almost upright, each leaf is 2.5–3m long, with narrow, 60cm long, greyish-green leaflets. Leaves are borne on thick, wide, short stalks, about 30cm in length. These petioles have a base that expands into a large, plump, and broadly triangular sheath, which is covered in a whitish sheen.

Dypsis decaryi produce infloresences of small, yellowish-green blossoms, and flower year-round. Each infloresence is 90–150cm

Opposite page
Dypsis decaryi
Triangle palms

Above
Dypsis decaryi
Triangle palm fruits

long and protrudes from the axils of the lower leaves. The triangle palm is a monoecious tree and its flowers are unisex. This means that the tree has separate male and female flowers, both borne on the same plant. As flowers fade they are followed by tiny ovoid fruits, each only 2.5cm long. The fruits are green to yellow when they first emerge, ripening to white or black as they mature.

Care: *Dypsis decaryi* palms should be planted in fertile, moist, well-drained soil enhanced with fertilizer. During the growing season, these trees need to be watered freely, and require an application of a balanced liquid fertilizer every six to eight weeks. Triangle palms are robust trees that can endure high temperatures and strong summer winds. Their placement in the garden is flexible, as they thrive in both direct sunlight and partial shade.

Propagation: From seed. Seeds should be cleaned and allowed to dry completely before planting. Typical germination time is 90 days; dry seeds will germinate more successfully than moist ones.

Pests and diseases: Palms in the *Dypsis* genus are susceptible to lethal yellowing disease. This affliction should be treated by a licensed exterminator.

Uses: The leaves of the triangle palm are used for roof thatching. The fruits of *Dypsis decaryi* are edible, high in nutritional protein, and can be consumed by people and used as livestock fodder. These fruits can also be made into a fermented drink.

This versatile tree is suited to most landscapes; an attractive addition to a formal garden, or placed in a container on a patio.

Opposite page and above
Dypsis decaryi
Triangle palms

Elaeis guineensis
African Oil Palm

The genus *Elaeis* is composed of two species of single-stemmed, pinnate-leaved palms. These monoecious plants are indigenous to the tropical regions of Africa but are widespread in tropical America and Southeast Asia. Commonly called oil palms, these trees are prized for the valuable oil extracted from the fruits of both species. Oil from palms in the *Elaeis* genus is one of the most widely used vegetable oils in the world.

***Elaeis guineensis*, African oil palm, macaw-fat palm:** The African oil palm is an erect, medium-sized, slow-growing tree. Reaching a mature height of 8–30m the stem of this palm, 30–60cm in diameter and covered in spent, fibrous leaf bases, supports a rounded leaf crown measuring 5–9m wide. This dense crown is composed of arching, large, pinnate leaves, 2.5–5m long. Each frond has a stout, green petiole, 90–150cm in length, bearing long, fibrous spines. The petiole supports 50–150 pendent, crowded, slender, linear, rich green pairs of leaflets, 60–120cm in length. Young African oil palms produce about 30 leaves a year; as the palm matures leaf growth slows, with established palms producing about 20 leaves over a 10-year period.

Elaeis guineensis, also known as the macaw-fat palm, flowers intermittently year-round. Three-petalled, yellow flowers grow on separate male and female panicles, although each tree produces both male and female blossoms. Flower panicles are 30–45cm long, emerging from the palm's leaf axils. Female flowers are followed by large, rounded bunches of ovoid fruits, each 2–5cm long, densely packed into clusters 30cm wide. The palm fruit takes five to six months to develop from pollination to maturity; fruits are initially green in color, ripening to orange or red and finally black. Each fruit is made up of an oily, fleshy outer layer, with a single seed, also rich in oil. The average African oil palm produces 10–15 fruit clusters at a time, each consisting of about 200 fruits.

Care: *Elaeis guineensis* palms should be planted in fertile, moist, well-drained soil enhanced with fertilizer. During the growing season, these trees need to be watered freely, and require an application of a balanced liquid fertilizer monthly. African oil palms are robust trees that can endure high temperatures and strong summer winds, although to truly flourish they require a humid climate. Their placement in the garden is flexible, as they thrive in both direct sunlight and partial shade.

Opposite page
Elaeis guineensis
African oil palm

Propagation: From seed. Prepare seeds for planting by soaking them in water for seven days. Seeds should be sown in spring; patience is required, however, as germination is a slow process.

Pests and diseases: African oil palms are susceptible to red spider mite, palm weevil, and many types of fungi. These pests should be treated by a licensed exterminator.

Uses: Palm fronds and seeds from *Elaeis guineensis* are processed for use as livestock feed, although this plant's most valuable product is its oil. The oil, extracted from fruits and seeds, is a valuable commodity in the international market. It is used in the manufacture of many products, such as margarine and cooking fats, as well as in making ice cream, mayonnaise, detergent, soap, and candles. Medicinally, oil from this palm is a folk remedy for treating headaches, rheumatism, and even cancer. Industrially, the oil is used as a lubricant in textile and rubber factories.

For landscaping purposes, a wide open space is ideal for this attractive palm. Clusters of three or more of these trees will stand out handsomely in any large garden.

Opposite page
Elaeis guineensis
African oil palm leaves

Above
Elaeis guineensis
African oil palm flowers

Hyphaene thebaica
Doum Palm

The genus *Hyphaene* is composed of approximately 10 species of palmate-leaved, dioecious plants. Native to the Arabian Peninsula, eastern and southern Africa, and Madagascar, most species in this genus are clustering palms, although some are single-trunked trees. Commonly named doum palms, these trees are usually stem-less, though some have creeping stems, and still others are tree-like with branching trunks. Newer growth covers the trunk in Y-shaped leaf bases; as these bases age they fall away and the trunk develops closely ringed scars. This genus is unique in that it has species with trunks that are naturally dichotomously branched. The trunk supports a leaf crown that is usually hemispherical, although dead leaves hanging beneath the crown give it a spherical appearance. Palms in the *Hyphaene* genus are moderate to large in size, with a few small-statured varieties.

***Hyphaene thebaica*, doum palm, gingerbread palm:** A medium-sized, slow-growing tree, the doum palm has a uniquely Y-shaped trunk, easily recognizable by the dichotomy of its stem forming two crowns. These two main crowns may then divide again into as many as eight to 16 crowns. Individual trunks within the tree grow to an average height of 6–10m (with a maximum height of 15m), range in girth from 30–90cm, and support a crown spreading 6–10m wide. The trunk is covered in fairly smooth, dark grey bark, and is scarred with leaf bases, which break up into fibers near the base of the trunk.

The dense crowns of the doum palm are composed of spirally arranged leaves, with eight to 20 leaves per crown. These leaves are palmate or fan-shaped, grey-green or silver-green in color, and have long, spiny-leafed stalks. Each petiole is 60–140cm in length, and supports numerous rounded leaf blades. Among the foliage is nestled tiny, bow-shaped, three-petalled, yellow or white flowers. *Hyphaene thebaica* is a dioecious plant, producing male and female flowers on separate trees. These blossoms are borne in panicles, up to 1m long, mainly in summer.

Doum palms with female flowers go on to produce large, woody, edible fruits. Measuring 8cm long, these oval or pear-shaped fruits are light or shiny brown when ripe, and remain on the tree for a long period of time. Each fruit contains a single seed. *Hyphaene thebaica* takes its other common name, gingerbread palm, from the taste of these fruits.

Care: *Hyphaene* palms are hardy trees that can endure high temperatures and strong summer winds. Their placement in the garden is flexible, as they thrive in both direct sunlight and partial shade. Doum palms should be planted in fertile, moist, well-drained soil enhanced with fertilizer. During the growing season, these trees need to be watered freely, and require an application of a balanced liquid fertilizer every six to eight weeks. Palms in the *Hyphaene* genus are most successful in humid climates, although they should be protected from extremely wet conditions.

Opposite page
Hyphaene thebaica
Doum palms

Right
Hyphaene thebaica
Doum palms

Propagation: From seed. Seeds should be sown in spring, and typically take 90 days to germinate, although germination may occur within 180 days or longer.

Pests and diseases: Doum palms are susceptible to red spider mite damage. These pests should be treated by a licensed exterminator.

Uses: All parts of the *Hyphaene thebaica* palm are useful. The tree often houses beehives, and timber from the trunk is used for posts and poles, in furniture production, and as wood for fuel. Dried bark is used to produce a black dye for leatherwear. The most widely used part of the tree, however, is the palm's leaves. Fiber and leaflets from the tree are used by people along the Niger and Nile rivers to weave baskets, mats, coarse textiles, brooms, ropes, string, and thatch. The leaf stalks are used for fencing, and the fiber is used for textiles and in the making of sponges and brushes. Other products made from the fronds include fishing rafts, brooms, hammocks, and carpets. Seeds from the fruits are made into buttons and beads.

Various parts of the doum palm are edible, and also have medicinal uses. The plant's fruit is edible, and the pulp can be chewed to control hypertension. The rind of the fruit can be ground to form a powder that is dried and added to food as a flavoring agent. The unripe kernels of the fruit are edible, and charcoal made from the seed kernel is used to treat sore eyes in livestock. Ground seeds can be made into a poultice for dressing wounds. Rind from the seeds is made into sweetmeats and molasses, and the shoots of germinated seeds are eaten as vegetables. The roots of this tree are used in the treatment of Bilharzia, a parasitic infection. In arid regions, the doum palm serves as fodder for livestock, particularly during periods of drought.

Hyphaene thebaica is a striking tree, and makes an eye-catching addition to any garden landscape. These trees may also be planted in groups in large, open spaces.

Above
Hyphaene thebaica
Doum palm fruits

Licuala grandis
Ruffled Fan Palm

Native to Malaysia, Australia and the southern and eastern regions of Asia and the Pacific Islands, the genus *Licuala* is composed of about 135 species of single- or cluster-stemmed palm trees. Palms in this genus range from 3–12m in height, and spread to widths of between 1.5 and 5m. Larger varieties of this plant are suitable for lawn specimens or in courtyards, while smaller species make attractive container plants, and may be grown indoors.

Licuala grandis, **ruffled fan palm:** Originating in the Solomon Islands and Vanuatu, the ruffled fan palm is a slow-growing species, reaching a mature height of 3m and spreading to a width of 1.5–2.5m. It has a single, slender, erect trunk which spreads to an average girth of 8cm. This trunk is covered in fibrous leaf bases from withered leaves. The plant gets its common name, ruffled fan palm, from its fan-like or palmately lobed leaves. These leaves are a glossy, mid- to deep green in color, and are arranged spirally along the upper parts of the stem. They are large, approximately 1m in diameter, with notched margins. Some varieties have fronds which are divided into three broadly wedge-shaped to rounded, wavy-margined segments.

In summer, *Licuala grandis* produces cup-shaped, three-petalled, yellowish-white flowers. These tiny blossoms, only 1cm in diameter, emerge from the leaf axils in pendent spikes which can be longer than the leaves of the palm. The flowers are followed by spherical, glossy red fruit.

Care: *Licuala palms* are resilient trees that can handle the harsh Arabian Gulf climate. They thrive when planted in direct sunlight, and are not adversely affected by high temperatures or strong summer winds. To truly flourish, these plants require moist, well-drained soil, enhanced with fertilizer. They are most successful when planted in an area with humid conditions.

Propagation: From seed, or by separating suckers from mature plants.

Pests and diseases: Plants in the *Licuala* genus are susceptible to red spider mite and mealy bug damage. These pests should be treated by a licensed exterminator.

Opposite page
Licuala grandis
Ruffled fan palm

Above
Licuala grandis
Ruffled fan palm flowers and fruits

Livistona chinensis
Chinese Fan Palm, Fountain Palm

Livistona is a genus composed of approximately 28 species of dioecious, large, single-stemmed palms. Native to tropical and sub-tropical regions of the world, plants in this genus range from 12–30m in height, and spread to widths of between 5 and 8m. Featuring palmate, or fan-shaped, leaves, most species have leaf segments that are rigid or shallow when young, growing pendulous as the plant ages.

When in bloom, *Livistona* palms produce inflorescences that emerge among the leaf crown. These spikes are branched twice or more, and bear bisexual flowers that produce blue, green, black, or brown fruits. Trees in this genus are commonly grown as specimen plants.

***Livistona chinensis*, Chinese fan palm, fountain palm:** Native to China, Japan and Taiwan, the Chinese fan palm is a slow-growing, medium-sized tree. When mature, this plant ranges in height from 12–15m, and spreads to a width of 4.5–5.5m. *Livistona chinensis* features a single, slender, erect, robust trunk, measuring 20–45cm in diameter and swollen at the base. The trunk of young trees is brown to reddish brown, and the upper part is covered with fibrous leaf bases. Older trees have a grey trunk marred by indistinct, closely set rings of leaf base scars.

Also known as the fountain palm, *Livistona chinensis* features a densely packed leaf crown composed of between 40 and 60 glossy, olive green leaves. These usually full and almost round, fan-shaped leaves measure 1.8m wide, and are divided for up to two-thirds of their length into 75 linear, pendent segments. The leaves rest on petioles 1.8–2m long; in younger palms the leaf stalks have toothed margins.

Chinese fan palms bloom in summer, producing cup-shaped, three-petalled, cream-colored flowers. These blossoms are borne in dramatic panicles measuring 1m or longer. The flowers are followed by spherical, glossy, blue-green to grey-pink fruit, 2–2.5cm in diameter.

Care: *Livistona chinensis* palms are resilient trees that can handle the harsh Arabian Gulf climate. Small specimens look great in pots and planters, and outdoors this tree is a nice choice for small gardens. They thrive when planted in direct sunlight, although young palms benefit from a location which receives partial shade. Fountain palms are not adversely affected by high temperatures or strong summer winds. To truly flourish, these plants require moist, well-drained soil enhanced with fertilizer. During the growing season, water freely and apply a balanced liquid fertilizer monthly. Fountain palms are most successful when planted in an area with humid conditions.

Propagation: From seed. Sow seeds in the springtime. Seedlings usually appear within 90 days, unless seeds were allowed to dry out before planting, in which case germination may be delayed.

Pests and diseases: *Livistona chinensis* is susceptible to lethal yellowing disease, red spider mite and scale insect damage. All of these afflictions should be treated by a licensed exterminator.

Opposite page
Livistona chinensis
Chinese fan palm

Right
Livistona chinensis
Chinese fan palms

Left
Livistona chinensis
Chinese fan palm
trunk, flowers and fruits

Phoenix
Palmae

The genus *Phoenix* includes approximately 15 species of palm trees, some solitary and some clumping. This genus contains both small and large trees, with varieties ranging in height from 2–30m and spreading to a width of between 2 and 12m. Their variety makes them attractive and interesting landscape specimens.

Native to tropical and subtropical regions around the world, *Phoenix* palms are found extensively in Africa, the Middle East, Asia, the Philippines, and Indonesia. The trunks of these palms are known for their rough texture and diamond-shaped scars. Trees in the *Phoenix* genus have pinnate leaves with induplicate folds, meaning the "v" of each fold faces skyward. They have linear to ovate or oblong leaflets which are reduced to long, stiff spines near the base of the leaf. *Phoenix* palms produce panicles of bowl-shaped, three-petalled, cream to yellow flowers, emerging from the plant's lower axils. As the flowers fade, they are followed by yellow, orange, red, brown, or black fruits.

The following are the most common *Phoenix* species grown in the Arabian Gulf region:

Phoenix canariensis, Canary Island date palm: Native to the Canary Islands, from which it takes its common name, this tree is a medium-sized, slow growing palm with a stout, columnar trunk. These plants reach a mature height of 15–20m, although usually shorter in cultivation, and spread to a width of 12m. The trunk of the tree ranges in girth from 60–150cm, is marked with oblong leaf scars, wider than they are long, and is light or dark brown in color. Young trees have bulbous trunks, almost pineapple-like in shape, and are covered with persistent, large, triangular leaf bases. Mature trees have smoother trunks, almost free of leaf bases except below the leaf crown, with the bottom 30cm or so of the trunk covered in short root initials.

Canary Island date palms feature a densely packed, immense leaf crown composed of over 100–150 pinnate leaves. These fronds are spreading to broadly arching, spiny, 4–6m in length, and consist of up 200 v-shaped linear, stiff, straight, bright mid-green to deep green leaflets, set in a single plane. *Phoenix canariensis* is a dioecious species; male plants have more flat-topped crowns and shorter leaves, while female trees have more rounded crowns and longer leaves.

From March to May, Canary Island date palms produce pendant panicles of small, bowl-shaped, cream to yellow, unisex flowers. Each panicle is 1–2m long, with many deep yellow to light orange single branches. After flowering, this tree bears cylindrical to ellipsoid, yellow to orange fruits, about 2cm long and 1cm in diameter. These edible fruits contain a single seed and have almost dry flesh. Although sweet, they are not very palatable.

Care: *Phoenix canariensis* are resilient trees that can withstand the harsh Arabian Gulf climate. They thrive when planted in direct

Opposite page
Phoenix canariensis
Canary Island date palm

sunlight, and are not adversely affected by high temperatures or strong summer winds. To truly flourish, these plants require moist, well-drained soil, enhanced with fertilizer. Canary Island date palms should be fertilized three times per year, with iron and manganese in water-soluble form. They are most successful when planted in an area with humid conditions. This tree is not self-cleaning; spent fronds must be manually removed.

Propagation: From seed, or by separating suckers from mature plants. Fresh seeds germinate two to three months after planting.

Pests and diseases: *Phoenix canariensis* palms are susceptible to red spider mite and palmetto weevil (*Rhynchophorus cruentatus*) damage. Palmetto weevils lay their eggs in the petioles of older leaves. The larvae burrow into the heart of the palm, eventually killing it. These pests should be treated by a licensed exterminator.

Uses: Canary Island date palms are often planted as ornamental trees in streets, parks and leisure areas throughout the Mediterranean region and in southwest Europe. In the Canary Islands, sap from this palm is used to make palm syrup, and the leaves are used for weaving baskets and other utensils.

Above
Phoenix canariensis
Canary Island date palm fruits

Opposite page
Phoenix canariensis
Canary Island date palm flowers

***Phoenix roebelenii**, pygmy date palm, miniature date palm:** *Phoenix roebelenii* is a dwarf species in the *Phoenix* genus, commonly known as the miniature date palm. This small tree grows to a mature height of only 1.8–3.6m, spreads to a width of 2.5m, and has a trunk measuring 15–20cm in diameter. Its diminutive size makes it a nice container plant, perfect for placement at the entrance of a home. Miniature date palms have a trunk whose base is wider than its top, and this trunk is often skirted with dead leaves. These clustering palms have foliage consisting of pinnate, slighting arching, pendant, deep green fronds. Each leaf is 1–1.2m in length, and is composed of many linear leaflets which sometimes have flattened, scale-like hairs on their undersides. In summer, miniature date palms produce panicles of bowl-shaped, creamy white flowers. These panicles, growing up to 45cm long, are followed by ellipsoid, edible black fruit, with each date measuring up to 1cm in length.

Care: Miniature date palms are hardy plants that flourish in direct sunlight. They are able to survive high temperatures, up to 50°C, and can also tolerate strong winds, as well as ground with a high saline content. *Phoenix roebelenii* should be planted in fertile, moist, well-drained, humus-rich soil, and do best in humid conditions. These plants need ample water and fertilizer to grow and thrive, and require special care to produce high-quality fruit.

Propagation: From seed.

Pests and diseases: Miniature date palms are susceptible to scale insects. These pests should be treated by a licensed exterminator.

Uses: *Phoenix roebelenii* are most commonly used as ornamental plants.

Opposite page
Phoenix roebelenii
Miniature date palms

Above
Phoenix roebelenii
Miniature date palm trunk, flowers and fruits at various stages of growth

Right
Phoenix sylvestris
Wild date palm

***Phoenix sylvestris**, **wild date palm, toddy palm, silver date palm:** Native to Pakistan, Sri Lanka, Nepal, Burma, Bangladesh, and most of India, *Phoenix sylvestris* is one of the most popular palm trees in the world. Known by the common names toddy palm, wild date palm, silver date palm, and sugar date palm, this tree grows to a mature height of 15–21m and spreads to a width of 9–10m. Its solitary trunk is 20–45cm in diameter, and supports a dense, round canopy packed with as many as 100 leaves. The trunk of younger trees is marred by triangular-shaped leaf scars which become more diamond-shaped with age. On older trees, the base of the trunk has aerial roots.

The common name of silver date palm probably refers to this tree's attractive, silvery green foliage. *Phoenix sylvestris* has gently arching, pinnately compound, waxy greyish- to bluish-green fronds. Each leaf can grow 2.5–3m long, and is borne on spiny petioles measuring 45cm in length. Leaves are composed of stiff leaflets, 45cm long, that grow opposite to one another on the rachis in such a way that the entire leaf looks flat.

Wild date palms begin flowering in early January, and stay in bloom through April. This tree produces unisex, small, whitish blossoms, borne on yellow branches, emerging in pendent inflorescences growing 90–100cm long. *Phoenix sylvestris* is a dioecious plant, with male and female flowers blooming on different trees. Male trees are extremely allergenic because their pollen is air-borne, whereas female palms cause minimal to no allergies.

After flowering, large, wide, pendent clusters of orange fruits emerge. These small, oblong fruits measure 1–2.5cm in length, and ripen to a purplish-red or black color. The fruits take almost a year to mature; they begin to ripen during the first week of June, and continue until the middle of July. Each fruit contains a single seed surrounded by a thin layer of flesh. Wild date fruits are edible, and have a sweet taste.

Above
Phoenix sylvestris
Wild date palm fruits

Right
Phoenix sylvestris
Wild date palm

Care: *Phoenix sylvestris* are hardy palms that flourish in direct sunlight. They are able to survive high temperatures, up to 50°C, and can also tolerate strong winds, as well as ground with a high saline content. Silver date palms should be planted in fertile, moist, well-drained, humus-rich soil, enhanced with palm fertilizer. These plants require ample water to grow and thrive, and are most successful in humid conditions. *Phoenix sylvestris* needs occasional trimming, so that old leaves do not form a skirt around the tree.

Propagation: From seed. Prepare seeds by removing the surrounding flesh and soaking them in warm water for one to three days. Germination occurs within one month.

Pests and diseases: *Phoenix sylvestris* is susceptible to lethal yellowing disease and mite damage. These afflictions should be treated by a licensed exterminator.

Uses: All parts of the *Phoenix sylvestris* palm are useful. The tree is a major source of sugar in India, hence its common name of sugar date palm. Its sap can be drunk fresh or fermented into a drink called toddy, giving the tree another common name, the toddy palm. In the West Bengal state of India, and in Bangladesh, the fresh sap is boiled to make palm jaggery. The leaves of the silver date palm are used for making mats, bags, fans, and brooms, and the fruit is used to make jelly.

Medicinally, wild date palm fruit, mixed with almonds, quince seeds, pistachio nuts, and sugar, is consumed as a restorative remedy. The flesh of the fruit is cooling, and is recommended for addressing heart complaints, abdominal issues, fever, vomiting and loss of consciousness. The central, tender part of the plant is used in the treatment of gonorrhea, and the roots are used to ease toothache.

For landscaping purposes, *Phoenix sylvestris* is an excellent street tree. It is used on golf courses, and in luxury neighborhoods for avenue planting. Young silver date palms make attractive container plants. When placing indoors, plant the tree in a deep pot that provides plenty of room for the taproot. Situate the palm in an area that receives plenty of light.

Ravenala madagascariensis
Traveller's Palm, Traveller's Tree

Native to Madagascar, the genus *Ravenala* consists of only one species of evergreen. Although this tree's trunk and leaves strongly resemble that of other palm plants, members of the *Ravenala* genus are not actually palms at all, belonging instead to the *Strelitziaceae* family (of which the bird of paradise is also a member).

***Ravenala madagascariensis*, traveller's palm, traveller's tree:** Grown primarily as a specimen plant, the traveller's palm is a large, erect tree known for its unusual foliage. Reaching a height of 10–16m and spreading to a width of 3–6m, this striking tree has an un-branched, palm-like trunk. Young traveller's palms have a subterranean trunk, which gradually emerges as the tree matures. This trunk is topped by a fan-shaped symmetrical crown of large, alternate, banana-like leaves. These lustrous, rich green leaves are long-stalked, two-ranked, paddle-shaped, and leathery in texture. Each leaf is composed of oblong leaf-blades, measuring 3–6m in length. The blades sprout from thick, grooved stalks, all of which are equal in length and closely overlap at their bases.

When in bloom, *Ravenala madagascariensis* produces multitudes of tiny, narrow white or green flowers. Each blossom has six tepals, which emerge from pointed, boat-shaped, greenish-white spathes, enclosing cymes, up to 30.5cm long. The flowers bloom from the leaf axils, a few at a time, throughout the summer. As the season fades, this tree produces brown fruit capsules that contain bright blue seeds.

Opposite page
Ravenala madagascariensis
Traveller's palm

Above
Ravenala madagascariensis
Traveller's palm trunk and flower

Right
Ravenala madagascariensis
Traveller's palm leaves

Caution: Parts of the plant are poisonous if ingested.

Care: Due to its height, traveller's palm is grown exclusively as an outdoor plant. Position the traveller's palm in a garden location receiving full sun, but also in a place sheltered from strong winds. Water regularly. This tree can be planted in any kind of soil, sandy or muddy, and is not effected by ground with a high-saline content. However, it is important that the soil be enriched with NPK fertilizer once a month. NPK is a chemical fertilizer consisting of nitrogen-potassium-phosphorus (10-10-10), which ensures that the plant is receiving enough nitrogen.

Propagation: From seed, or by separating rooted suckers from mature traveller's palm plants in the spring.

Pests and diseases: This tree is susceptible to red spider mite damage. These pests should be treated by a licensed exterminator.

Uses: The scientific name of the genus *Ravenala* comes from the Malagasy word *ravinala* meaning "forest leaves" (Malagasy is the national language of Madagascar). The leaves of this tree were used traditionally by people travelling in the forest as sheathes to hold rainwater for drinking in case of emergencies; hence its common name, traveller's palm.

Above
Ravenala madagascariensis
Traveller's palm flowers

Rhapis excelsa
Broadleaf Lady Palm, Bamboo Palm

Native to China and Taiwan, the *Rhapis* genus includes 12 species of small, cluster-stemmed palms. Known by the common name lady palm, these trees feature foliage composed of thin stems supporting palmate leaves with a bare petiole, terminating in a rounded fan of numerous leaflets. Plants in the *Rhapis* genus reach an average of 1.5–5m in height, branching at the base, forming clumps.

Rhapis excelsa (synonym *Rhapis flabelliformis*), **broadleaf lady palm, bamboo palm:** A small, multi-stemmed tree, the broadleaf lady palm grows to a mature height and width of 1.5–5m. It has slender, erect, bamboo- or reed-like stems, each with a diameter of only 2.5cm. These stems support foliage consisting of wiry stalks, 20–45cm long, bearing circular, palmate leaves with narrow, ribbed, dark green segments. The number of leaf segments increase as the plant ages; young plants may have only one or a few, while mature plants may have a dozen or more. New foliage emerges from a fibrous sheath which remains attached to the base of the palm. As the plant gets older these sheaths are shed.

Like all palms in the *Rhapis* genus, *Rhapis excelsa* is a dioecious tree, with male and female flowers produced on separate plants. Blossoms are borne in panicles measuring up to 12cm in length, nestled between the leaves or at the top of the palm. These tiny, cream or yellowish-white, bowl-shaped, three-petalled flowers are fused at the base. They emerge in summer, and are followed by fleshy fruit that is white when ripe.

Care: *Rhapis* palms should be placed in a shaded area of the garden. They require reasonably fertile, moist, well-drained soil. Outside of the growing season these plants need only moderate watering. During the growing season, however, they should be watered freely, and given a monthly application of a balanced liquid fertilizer.

Opposite page
Rhapis excelsa
Broadleaf lady palms

Above
Rhapis excelsa
Broadleaf lady palm fruits

Right
Rhapis excelsa
Broadleaf lady palm leaves

Propagation: *Rhapis excelsa* is most easily propagated by division, in springtime. This plant produces underground rhizome offshoots. It can also be propagated by seed; seeds will germinate within four months.

Pests and diseases: Palms in the *Rhapis* genus are susceptible to red spider mite, scale insect and mealy bug damage. All of these pests should be treated by a licensed exterminator.

Uses: Various parts of the *Rhapis excelsa* palm are used in traditional medicine to treat many different ailments, including infectious diseases. The bark can be charred and applied to external wounds to stop bleeding. Decoctions from the ashes of burnt bark and roots are said to stimulate blood circulation and are a treatment for rheumatism. The fibrous, inner part of the basal section of the leaf stalk is used in Chinese medicine.

For landscaping purposes, the bamboo palm can be used in the garden in shady borders, or to add foliage variety to a group of plantings. *Rhapis excelsa* is also an excellent choice for a houseplant. In fact, this palm was listed by NASA as one of the best plants for removing toxins from indoor air.

Above
Rhapis excelsa
Broadleaf lady palms

Roystonea regia
Royal Palm

Roystonea is a genus of 10 species of solitary-trunked, pinnate-leaved, monoecious palms. Native to south Florida, Cuba, Central and northern South America, palms in this genus resemble each other closely, and are often hard for lay gardeners to identify. These trees are identified by their inflorescence shape, flower color, and fruit characteristics.

***Roystonea regia*, royal palm:** Reaching a mature height of 25–30m, and spreading 6–10m wide, *Roystonea regia* is considered by many to be the world's most beautiful palm. This striking tree has an eye-catching trunk. It is swollen at the base, constricts about half way up, and then bulges again just below the crownshaft, which is emerald green and measures 1.8–2m tall. The trunk ranges from 37–60cm in diameter, is smooth, light grey to white in color, and is distinctly ringed in its younger parts with darker leaf base scars.

The majestic trunk of the royal palm supports a nearly spherical leaf crown of 15–20 leaves. Each leaf is 3–5m long and consists of many linear, deep green leaflets. These leaflets are 60–120cm long, and are arranged in rows. This foliage serves as a contrast for the tree's tiny, cup-shaped, three-petalled, creamy white to creamy yellow flowers. Blooming in summer, these flowers are borne in panicles, 1m long and 1m wide, which emerge just below the crownshaft. *Roystonea regia* produces round fruits, initially green and ripening from red to purplish-black.

Care: *Roystonea* palms should be placed in an area of the garden that receives full sunlight. They require reasonably fertile,

Opposite page
Roystonea regia
Royal palm

Above
Roystonea regia
Royal palm flowers

Right
Roystonea regia
Royal palms

moist, well-drained soil. Outside of the growing season these plants need only moderate watering. During the growing season, however, they should be watered freely, and given a monthly application of a balanced liquid fertilizer. Properly irrigated, the trunk of the tree can grow up to 30cm per year.

Royal palms are considered self-cleaning trees; spent leaves will shed neatly from the tree at a rate of about one leaf per month. This makes the palm easy to maintain. Care should be taken when considering its placement in the garden, however, as leaves can cause injury to people and damage to property when they fall.

Propagation: From seed. Seeds should be freshly collected from ripe fruits, in springtime. Prepare seeds for planting by removing any fleshy pulp and soak the seeds in water for five days. Rubber gloves should be worn when handling the fruits of *Roystonea regia*, since the pulp contains calcium oxalate crystals that are highly irritating to exposed skin.

Once prepared, sow seeds in well-drained, uniformly moist potting soil and keep warm. Germination will occur anywhere from 30 to as many as 180 days after planting. After germination, place seedlings in a cool area out of direct sunlight. Seedlings will be grass-like in appearance. The first leaves that emerge will look different from the ones that follow; seedlings should be transplanted into containers after the second leaf emerges.

Pests and diseases: Plants in the *Roystonea* genus are susceptible to red spider mite, scale insect and mealy bug damage. These pests should be treated by a licensed exterminator.

Uses: *Roystonea regia* is the national tree of Cuba. Wood from the tree is used in construction, and the leaves are used for thatching. This tree serves as a roosting site and food source for a variety of animals. Its flowers attract birds and bats, who eat its fruit, and the fruit is also used as livestock fodder. The seeds of this tree are a source of oil.

Roystonea regia is also known as a medicinal plant. The roots are a natural diuretic, and are used in the treatment of diabetes.

For landscaping purposes, royal palms make beautiful lawn specimens, and are attractive additions to large gardens. They closely resemble the Foxtail palm (*Wodyetia bifurcata*), but grow larger in size. *Roystonea regia* is also a popular choice for landscaping public areas such as streets, parks, and commercial properties.

Above
Roystonea regia
Royal palm leaves and flowers

Sabal palmetto
Cabbage Palm, Sabal Palm

Sabal is a small genus composed of approximately 14 species of palms. They have an extensive indigenous region, from the West Indies to the southern United States, and from northern South America through Central America. These single-stemmed or stem-less palm trees vary in height from 1–30m, and can reach a spread of 7m, depending on the species.

***Sabal palmetto*, cabbage palm, sabal palm:** *Sabal palmetto* is a species of large, slow-growing, versatile, evergreen tree. Reaching a height of 20–30m, and spreading 5–7m wide, cabbage palms have a rough trunk, approximately 30–60cm in width, and a distinctive foliage growth pattern. The cabbage palm has no crownshaft; leaves emerge directly from the trunk. Leaf bases are sometimes retained on the trunk and form a skirt below the crown, with the stalks in a criss-cross pattern. Cabbage palms have short, bulbous root systems, penetrating the soil to depths of 4.6–6.1m.

Sabal palmetto trees have fronds consisting of compact, spherical heads of numerous fan-shaped, rich green leaves. These leaves, around 1.5–2m in length, are deeply divided into 40–60, two-lobed leaflets. Each leaflet, averaging 80cm in length, is split to about half the width of the leaf. It has thread-like filaments hanging between the leaflets, and sheds tan fibers at the edges. The fronds have a bare petiole (leafstalk) which extends as a center spine or midrib (costa). Cabbage palms have fronds that are costapalmate in shape; the leaf has a distinct central midrib but the leaflets are arranged radially (fan-like) rather than pinnately (like a date palm). Each leaf has a bare stalk that extends to the center of the midrib. The leaflets of costapalmate leaves are always distinctly arched backwards.

In summer, cabbage palms produce tiny, creamy white, bisexual blossoms. These delicate three-petalled flowers, only 5mm in diameter, emerge in long panicles which can reach up to 2.5m, exceeding the surrounding leaves. The scent of the female flower is similar to that of the blooms of the Queen of the Night shrub (*Cestrum nocturnum*). The fragrant blossoms are pollinated by bees, and are followed by black, fleshy fruits. Each

Opposite page
Sabal palmetto
Cabbage palm

Above
Sabal palmetto
Cabbage palm flowers

Above
Sabal palmetto
Cabbage palm

fruit, growing to about 1.3cm long, contains a single hard, brown, spherical seed.

Care: Sabal palms thrive in garden locations where they receive full sun, with some midday shade. These plants are drought tolerant, and grow best in fertile, moist, well-drained soil.

Propagation: By seed. Germination is most successful when fresh seeds are used, and so is conducted in springtime, when the tree is bearing fruit. Seeds may sprout in as few as 18 days, and 50% of the final germination should occur within 33 days, although complete germination may take up to a year.

Pests and diseases: Cabbage palms are susceptible to red spider mite and scale insect damage. Both of these pests should be treated by a licensed exterminator.

Uses: The trunk of the sabal palm is used for dock support pilings, since they are salt tolerant and their flexible, fibrous nature allows them to move with the water. Young palm fronds can be made into brushes and brooms. Some parts of the sabal palm are even edible. Large leaf buds of immature trees, as well as the "heart" or core of the trunk, are used to make swamp cabbage and hearts-of-palm salad. The foliage has a cabbage-like flavor, hence the plant's common name, the cabbage palm. Harvesting the heart of the plant results in the death of the tree, however, so when purchasing heart of palm one should always check that the producer uses sustainable farming methods.

Various types of *Sabal* palms can serve different landscaping purposes; single-stemmed trees may be used as lawn specimens, while stem-less varieties make attractive shrub borders.

Above
Sabal palmetto
Cabbage palm
fruits and flowers

Washingtonia
Desert Fan

Native to southwestern North America, the genus *Washingtonia* is composed of five species of single-stemmed trees. These trees feature deeply lobed, fan-shaped leaves. The leaves grow in terminal heads that form a dense, shaggy skirt covering the trunk from top to bottom as they die back. Palms in this genus range from 15–30m in height, and spread to widths of between 2.5 and 6m.

The following are the most common *Washingtonia* species grown in the Arabian Gulf region:

Washingtonia filifera, desert fan: This tall, fast-growing palm tree can live for 80 to 250 years or more. The desert fan palm has a robust, columnar trunk that gradually tapers upward from ground level to the crown. *Washingtonia filifera* reach a mature height of 15–20m and spread to a width of 3–6m, with an average trunk girth of 90–120cm.

Washingtonia filifera features grey-green foliage consisting of wide, palmate leaves. These leaves are erect when young, arching with age. Each leaf has a curved, spiny stalk, 100–150cm in length, and a sharply-toothed base. From this stalk grows fan-shaped blades, 1.5–3m long, accounting for between one-third to one-half of the total length of the leaf. Each blade consists of 40–70 accordion-like folds, with the leaflets connected near the stalk and separating towards their tips. The long fibers hanging from the leaflets give this species its botanical name.

In summer, desert fan palms produce slender, arching panicles of tubular, creamy white,

Opposite page
Washingtonia sp.
Desert fans

Above
Washingtonia sp.
Desert fan flowers and fruits

bisexual flowers. Each flower has three-petaled lobes, and each panicle of blossoms can grow as long as 5m.

Washingtonia robusta, thread palm: Another tall, fast growing member of the *Washingtonia* genus, the thread palm quickly reaches its mature height of 25–30m, with a crown spreading 2.5–5m wide. This tree features a slender trunk, thinner than that of *Washingtonia filifera*, which gradually tapers from the ground level to the crown. The trunk is often ringed with spent fronds, forming a shaggy skirt at the base of the crown. The foliage of the thread palm is composed of sharply toothed, fan-shaped leaf-stalks. Each stalk supports bright green blades, measuring 1m in length. Fronds have an arching lobe tip, with inconspicuous or no filaments.

Washingtonia robusta blooms in summer, producing tubular, creamy pink flowers. Individual blossoms have three-petaled lobes, and the flowers are borne in slender, arching panicles, measuring 3m in length.

Care: *Washingtonia* palms are appropriate for Arabian Gulf gardens, as they thrive in full sun or partial shade and are tolerant of salty soil. They do, however, require frequent fertilization with a water-soluble fertilizer. These palms also need regular watering.

Propagation: From seed.

Pests and diseases: All of the plants in the *Washingtonia* genus are susceptible to red spider mite and scale insect damage. These pests should be treated by a licensed exterminator.

Uses: For landscaping purposes, *Washingtonia* palms are suitable for coastal gardens or along city streets.

Opposite page
Washingtonia sp.
Desert fans

Above
Washingtonia sp.
Desert fan leaf stalks

Wodyetia bifurcata
Foxtail Palm

Native to Queensland, Australia, *Wodyetia* is a genus of only one distinct species of palm tree. This solitary, attractive palm grows to a full height of 10–18m. Its columnar, slightly bottle-shaped trunk may be single, double, or even triple; its leaves fall naturally, leaving the trunk clean and smooth. The trunk is slim, averaging only 25cm in diameter, and is closely ringed with leaf scars. It is dark grey in color near the crownshaft, fading to light grey in the middle and finally turning white towards its slightly swollen base.

***Wodyetia bifurcata*, foxtail palm:** Bred by crossing *Washingtonia bifurcata* with *Veitchia joannis*, *Wodyetia bifurcata* gets its common name, the foxtail palm, from the bushy, foxtail-like plume of fronds that emerges from the tree's light to bright green crownshaft. Its compound, dark green to light green leaves measure 2–3m in length. They are pinnate, gracefully arching, and composed of leaflets that radiate out at all angles from the leaf stem. Foxtail palms are fully mature 12 years after planting, at which time they will have a canopy of eight to 10 leaves and a crown of foliage 4.6–6.1m across.

The foxtail is a flowering palm, with a heavily branched inflorescence bearing white to cream-colored blossoms. Blooming from late spring through early summer, it is a monoecious tree, with both male and female flowers emerging from the same stalk, which sprouts from the base of the tree's crownshaft. Once the flowers fade, they are followed by clusters of oval-globose, single-seeded fruits. These fruits, measuring about 5–6cm long and 3–4cm wide, emerge olive-green in color and ripen from orange to red.

Care: The foxtail palm is perfect for gardens in the Arabian Gulf region. It is a hardy, durable tree with a deep root system. It can tolerate moderate drought, salt spray, and

Opposite page
Wodyetia bifurcata
Foxtail palm

Above
Wodyetia bifurcata
Foxtail palm
fruits and leaves

high winds, and can grow in a variety of soils, from alkaline limestone to rocky sands. Foxtail palms are a great choice for novice gardeners, as they are exceptionally hardy and easy to care for. They thrive in locations receiving full sun, although they will also grow in partial sun or shade. *Wodyetia bifurcata* flourishes with consistent watering, well-drained soil, and regular fertilization with palm fertilizer. This tree should be pruned of dead fronds, however, as falling leaves may be a hazard to the public.

Propagation: From seed. Seeds must be fully mature and freshly collected. Prepare seeds for planting by removing them from the fruit and scarring the seed coat with a knife or scratching it with a file or sandpaper. Cover with soil, and place in a moist, humid location. Germination should occur within one to three months, though it may take up to one year. Seedlings should be transplanted during spring and summer.

Pests and diseases: Foxtail palms are susceptible to aphid, scale insect, and mealy bug damage. All of these pests should be treated by a licensed exterminator.

Uses: The foxtail palm is versatile, and can be used in a wide variety of landscape designs. It can be grown outdoors as a single specimen plant in small gardens, or in clusters in larger yards. Foxtail palms are often used by city landscapers, planted in lines along avenues to give an area a tropical look. These trees can even be grown indoors in containers, if given enough light and space. *Wodyetia bifurcata* is a regal tree, possessing one of the most spectacular foliage displays of all the palms.

Opposite page
Wodyetia bifurcata
Foxtail palm fruits

Above
Wodyetia bifurcata
Foxtail palm flowers

References

Abdullah, Fatima Mohammed (1993) *Shade and Ornamental Plants* (in Arabic), Al Khobar, Saudi Arabia: Tasheelat Publishing.

Abu Dahab, Mohammed (1992) *Ornamental Plants Production* (in Arabic), Riyadh: Dar al-Mareekh Publishing.

Abu Zayed, al-Shahhat Nasr (2002) *Planting and Production of Flowers and Ornamental Plants* (in Arabic), Egypt: al-Dar al-Arabia for Publishing and Distribution.

al-Ba'labaki, Moneer (1978) *al-Mawrid* (in Arabic), Beirut: Dar al-Ilm Lilmalayin.

al-Dajwi, Ali (2004) *Ornamental Plants Production: Garden and Flower Design* (in Arabic), Egypt: Madbouly Publishing.

al-Faisal, Prince Mohammed al-Abdullah (n.d.) *Nurseries Nowarah Farm Booklet: Alkharj Area, Southern Riyadh* (in Arabic).

al-Ghitani, Mohammed Yusri (1985) *Flowers and Ornamental Plants: Garden Design* (in Arabic), Egypt: al-Jamia al-Masriya Publishing.

al-Khazrajy, Ammar Salem (2008) *Medical Herbs Lexicon* (in Arabic), Beirut: Dar al-Hadi Publishing.

al-Najjar, Hussain (1987) *Ornamental Plants: Garden Design and Fruit Trees* (in Arabic).

al-Nasr, Mahmoud Hamdi Seif (1999) *Flowers and Ornamental Plants* (in Arabic).

al-Qae'ae, Tareq Mahmoud (1986) *Garden Design and Coordination* (in Arabic).

al-Qahtani, Jaber bin Salem (2008a) *Jaber's Herbal Medicine Encyclopedia – Part 1*, 2nd edition (in Arabic), Riyadh: Obeikan Publishing.

_____(2008b) *Jaber's Herbal Medicine Encyclopedia – Part 2*, 2nd edition (in Arabic), Riyadh: Obeikan Publishing.

_____(2009) *Jaber's Herbal Medicine Encyclopedia – Part 4*, 2nd edition (in Arabic), Riyadh: Obeikan Publishing.

al-Sayyed, Abd al-Baset Mohammed (2009) *Ninety Healing Herbs at the Perfumer's House: 127 Questions and 1000 Treatments* (in Arabic), Riyadh: al-Hadara Publishing and Distribution.

al-Shaer, Mahmoud al-Sayed (1998) *One Hundred Tips for Ornamental Plant Care: Issues, Treating During Travelling, Therapeutic Benefits* (in Arabic), Egypt: Dar al-Talae.

al-Sultan Gardens (n.d.) *Zaid al-Hussain Nurseries farm booklet* (in Arabic), Saudi Arabia.

Aqiel, Mohsen (2005) *Comic Herbs Lexicon* (in Arabic), Beirut: al-Aalami Publishing.

Bawden-Davis, Julie (2001) *Houseplants & Indoor Gardening: Decorating Your Home with Houseplants*, Minnetonka: Creative Pub. International.

_____(2004) *Flower Gardening: A Practical Guide to Creating Colorful Gardens in Every Yard*, Pleasantville: Reader's Digest.

Binney, Ruth (1987) *World Book Encyclopedia of Science: The Plant World*, Chicago: World Book, Inc.

Brickell, Christopher (2003) *The Royal Horticultural Society A-Z Encyclopedia of Garden Plants*, vols. 1 and 2, London: Dorling Kindersley.

_____(2007) *The Royal Horticultural Society Encyclopedia of Gardening*, 3rd ed. fully rev. and expanded, London: Dorling Kindersley.

_____(2010) *The Royal Horticultural Society Encyclopedia of Plants and Flowers*, fifth edition, London: Dorling Kindersley.

Carter, George, and Marianne Majerus (2000) *Living with Plants*, London: Mitchell Beazley.

Clausen, Ruth Rogers (1999) *Wildflowers, Fandex Family Field Guides*, New York: Workman Pub.

Cox, Martyn (2011) *Royal Horticultural Society: How to Grow Plants in Pots*, London: Dorling Kindersley.

Cullen, James, Sabina Knees and Suzanne Cubey (2011a) *The European Garden Flora I. Angiospermae – Monocotyledons. Alismataceae to Orchidaceae*, Cambridge: Cambridge University Press.

_____(2011b) *The European Garden Flora II. Angiospermae – Dicotyledons. Casuarinaceae to Cruciferae*, Cambridge: Cambridge University Press.

_____(2011c) *The European Garden Flora III. Angiospermae – Dicotyledons. Resedaceae to Cyrillaceae*, Cambridge: Cambridge University Press.

_____(2011d) *The European Garden Flora IV. Angiospermae – Dicotyledons. Aquifoliaceae to Hydrophyllaceae*, Cambridge: Cambridge University Press.

_____(2011e) *The European Garden Flora V. Angiospermae – Dicotyledons. Boraginaceae to Compositae*, Cambridge: Cambridge University Press.

Darwiesh, Emad (2001a) *Home Plants*, Section I, Part 9 (in Arabic), Damascus: Dar Dimashq for Publishing.

_____(2001b) *Home Plants*, Section II, Part 10 (in Arabic), Damascus: Dar Dimashq for Publishing.

Edinger, Philip, and John K. McClements (1990) *Garden Color: Annuals & Perennials*, Menlo Park, California: Sunset Publishing Corporation.

Ellis, Barbara W (1999) *Taylor's Guide to Annuals: How to Select and Grow More than 400 Annuals, Biennials, and Tender Perennials*, Boston: Houghton Mifflin Co.

Flower Council of Holland (2004) *Plants from Holland Naturally*, Lieden, Holland.

Friis, Anny (2003) *Australian House and Garden: Garden*, Sydney: Australian Consolidated Press.

Gardening Australia (May 2010), Alexandria: Federal Pub.

Green, Jane (1999) *Flowers for Riyadh Gardens*, London: Stacey International.

Gunter, Caroline (2001) *Truly Tiny Gardens*, Sydney: Australian Women's Weekly.

Hageneder, Fred (2005) *The Meaning of Trees: Botany, History, Healing, Lore*, San Francisco: Chronicle Books.

Hessayon, D.G. (2000) *The Garden Expert*, London: Expert Books.

_____(2001) *The Rock & Water Garden Expert*, London: Expert Books.

_____(2004) *The House Plant Expert*, London: Expert Books.

_____(2006) *The Flower Arranging Expert*, London: Expert Books.

_____(2007) *The Lawn Expert*, London: Expert Books.

_____(2009) *The Container Expert*, London; New York: Expert Books.

Humphries, C.J., Press, J.R. and Sutton, D.A. (1989) Reprinted (2009), *Hamlyn Guide to Trees of Britain and Europe*, London: Octopus Publishing Group Ltd.

Jefferson-Brown, Michael (1998) *The Easy Garden Month-by-Month*, Newton Abbot: David & Charles.

Jordan, Michael (2012) *The Beauty of Trees*, London: Quercus Editions Ltd.

Kroll, Sander (2005) *Feeling Good with Plants, Extra Large*, Amsterdam: Ki Plant Concept BV-Aalsmeer.

Lewis, Eleanore (2001) *Water Gardens*, Des Moines, Iowa: Better Homes and Gardens Books.

Martin, Tovah, and David Cavagnaro (1999) *Heirloom Flowers: Vintage Flowers for Modern Gardens*, New York: Fireside.

McHoy, Peter (2005) *How to Keep Houseplants Alive and Happy*, London: Southwater.

McIntyre, Anne (2002) *The Complete Floral Healer*, New York: Sterling.

Medlevant (1985) *Home Cultivation* (in Arabic).

Ministry of Awqaf and Islamic Affairs, Qatar (2018) *Qatar Calendar* (in Arabic).

Moore, Eric (2007) *Gardening in the Middle East [With Plant Encyclopaedia]*, London: Stacey International.

Municipality of Doha (2007) *Seasonal and Perennial Flowers in the State of Qatar*, Doha: Green Qatar Centre.

Phillips, Barty (2001) *Garden Design*, Bath: Parragon.

Rees, Yvonne, and Nick Fletcher (2002) *Indoor Water Garden Design*, Hauppauge, New York: Barron's Educational Series, Inc.

Riffle, Robert Lee (2008) *Timber Press Pocket Guide to Palms*, London: Timber Press, Inc.

Rosenfeld, Richard (2002) *The Summer Garden*, London: Lorenz.

Seif al-Nasr, Mahmoud Hamdi (1999) *Flowers and Ornamental Plants* (in Arabic), Egypt: al-Dar al-Masriya al-Lubnaniya.

Shaheen, Elizabeth (2003) *Exotic Perennials and Annuals for Pots in Bahrain*, Manama, Bahrain: Miracle Publishing.

Sheeha, Muneer Yusuf (1984) *Plant Entrepreneurship in Kuwait* (in Arabic).

Spence, Ian (2007) *The Royal Horticultural Society Gardening Month by Month*, London: Dorling Kindersley.

Turner, Katharina (1996) *Garden Design*, Bristol: Parragon.

van Dijk, Hanneke, and Mineke Kurpershoek (2001). *The Complete Encyclopedia of Bulbs and Tubers. An Expert Guide to the Most Beautiful Bulbous and Tuberous Plants*, Lisse, the Netherlands: Rebo Pub.

Walsh, Kevin (2010) *Waterwise Plants*, Chatswood, Australia: New Holland Publishers.

Warren, William, and Luca Invernizzi (2004) *Handy Pocket Guide to Tropical Flowers*, Singapore: Periplus Editions.

World Book, Inc. (1992 and 1993) *The World Book Encyclopedia*, vols. 1–21, Chicago: World Book.

Wyatt, Nancy Fitzpatrick, ed. (1998) *Southern Living Annuals and Perennials*, Birmingham, Alabama: Oxmoor House, Inc.

Yakeley, Diana, and Caroline Arber (2003) *Der Indoor-Garten: Wohndesign mit Pflanzen*, Munich: Callwey.

Young, Emily, and Dave Egbert (2007) *Big Ideas for Small Gardens*, Menlo Park, California: Sunset Publishing Corporation.

Zadah, Mortaza Akbar (2008) *Encyclopaedia of Herbs and Plants in the Qur'an and Sunnah: Benefits and Properties* (in Arabic), Beirut: al-Aalami Publishing.

Glossary

Aerial root: A root which grows out from the stem above ground level.

Air layering: a method of propagating single-stem plants which have lost their lower leaves.

Alternate: Used to describe a leaf form where the leaves are arranged singly at different heights on the stem.

Annual: A plant which completes its life-cycle from seed to seed in less than one year.

Apex: The tip; the distal end.

Auricle: An earlike lobe, a part of the leaf sheath or petiole.

Axil: The angle formed by the stem and the petiole.

Axillary: Situated in or arising from an axil.

Berry: Fleshy fruit without a stony layer surrounding the seeds.

Bi-pinnate: A pinnate leaf whose primary leaflets have been replaced by separate and smaller stalks that then bear their leaflets with or without individual stalks; twice compound. Often written as "two-pinnate."

Bisexual: Used to describe flowers that have both male and female parts.

Blade: Expanded, flattened part of a leaf.

Bloom: Whitish or bluish covering, easily removed.

Bonsai: The Japanese art of training, shaping, and pruning plants in containers to create a mini-naturized garden of dwarfing trees by careful root and stem pruning coupled with root restriction.

Bract: A structure (botanically, it is a modified leaf) borne below a flower or an inflorescence. Palm inflorescences usually have one or several to many bracts, which may be woody, leathery or papery in texture. Some plant bracts are colorful and mistaken for a petal.

Bud: Developing shoot or flower.

Calyx: The outer ring of flower parts, usually green but sometimes colored.

Columnar: Narrow, almost parallel-sided crown.

Compound leaf: A leaf made up of two or more leaflets attached to the leaf stalk.

Cone: Inflorescence of a conifer, often woody or conical, composed of scales and bract.

Conifer: Sometimes called evergreens, these are plants with needle-like foliage such as junipers, cypresses, pines, and cedars. All bear cones or cone-like seed structures.

Coniferous: Cone-bearing.

Corolla: Petals of a flower considered as a whole.

Corona: A crown, a circular appendage, or a circle of appendages in a flower.

Corymb: Short, broad, and more or less flat-topped inflorescence, developing like a raceme.

Costa: The projection of the petiole into the leaf blade (or lamina) of a costapalmate-leaved palm species.

Costapalmate: Said of palmate leaf with a discernible costa.

Crenate: Margin with shallow, rounded teeth.

Crownshaft: A term used only with pinnate-leaved palm species to denote a tubular or cylindrical shaft above the woody part of the trunk. The tube is more or less columnar and consists of the expanded and tightly packed leaf bases of the leaves presently on the palm.

Cultivar: A variety or form of a species that originates in cultivation and is not found naturally.

Cuttings: A method of propagating some plants by causing a section cut from the stem of the plant to develop roots of its own.

Cyme: A determinate inflorescence, usually broad or more or less flat-topped; the central or terminal flower opening first.

Deciduous: Non-evergreen; shedding leaves seasonally, thus leafless for part of the year.

Dioecious: Having male (staminate) and female (pistillate) flowers on separate plants.

Division: A method of propagating plants by separating each one into two or more sections, then re-potting.

Drainage: The rate at which water passes downward through the soil.

Drupe: A fleshy fruit with a stone-like shell containing the kernel or seed, such as a peach.

Endosperm: The storage tissue in the seed. It can be oily, such as the "meat" of a coconut, or very hard, such as the "ivory" of a *Phoenix dactylifera* seed.

Entire leaf: An undivided and un-serrated leaf, or a margin unbroken by teeth or lobes.

Evergreen: Having foliage that remains green and functional throughout more than one growing season.

Frond: A leaf of a fern or palm.

Fruit: Ripe seeds and surrounding structures, either fleshy or dry.

Genus: A collection of plants bearing similar characters. The category in scientific classification that ranks below family and above species.

Germination: The first stage in the development of a plant from seed.

Glabrous: Plant surface which is smooth, not hairy.

Gland: A small vesicle containing oil or other liquid, within, on or protruding from the surface of a plant.

Glaucous: Plant surface which is covered with a whitish or bluish bloom or a waxy or powdery substance that is easily rubbed away.

Globose: Globe-shaped body, more or less round in cross-section.

Grafting: The process of joining a stem or bud of one plant on to the stem of another.

Hastula: A flap of tissue on some palmate leaves. This flap is variously shaped and protrudes from the point at which the petiole joins the leaf blade. The protruding organ may be tiny or large and may be found on either the upper or lower surface of the leaf, or on both surfaces.

Herbaceous: A plant with a non-woody stem.

Hermaphrodite: Bearing bisexual flowers.

Humus: Soft brown or black material formed by the decomposition of animal or vegetable matter. In common landscape use, it is semi-decomposed plant matter–leaves, twigs, grass clippings, or sawdust used as a mulch or soil improvement.

Hybrid: A plant originating from the fertilization of one species by another.

Induplicate: The folding (plication) of the leaflet so that the margins are turned upwards and the leaflet has a v-shape in cross-section. The contrasting condition is *reduplicate*.

Inflorescence: The branch (and all accompanying bracts and subsidiary branches) that bears the flowers; the flower-bearing structure.

Juvenile: Young, first-formed.

Lanceolate: Lance-shaped. Having a shape that is longer than wide, with the widest part near the point of attachment.

Lateral: On or at the side.

Latex: Milky sap which exudes from cut surfaces of a plant.

Leaf base: The lowest or bottom part of a leaf. A widened (often greatly so) portion of the bottom of the leaf's stalk.

Leaflet: The individual segment of a pinnate leaf.

Legume: A dry fruit splitting along its length above and below to release its seeds; typically, the fruit of a species of the pea family.

Linear: Narrow and more or less parallel-sided.

Lobe: A major segment of an organ, representing a division to halfway to the middle of the organ, or less.

Midrib: The main veins(s) of a leaf or, as used in this volume, the central stalk of a pinnate leaf.

Monoecious: Having separate male and female flowers on a single plant.

Node: The point on a stem from which a leaf, a group of leaves, buds or flowers are attached.

Oblanceolate: Inversely lanceolate, with the broadest width above the middle, and tapering to the base.

Obovate: Inversely ovate; broader above, rather than below, the middle.

Obtuse: Blunt. Not sharp or pointed.

Operculum: Rounded cover or lid.

Opposite: Leaf form, where the leaves are arranged in opposite pairs along the stem.

Ovary: Female part of the flower immediately enclosing the ovule.

Ovate: Shaped like a hen's egg.

Ovoid: A solid body, wide below the middle, ovate in cross-section.

Palmate: Fan-like. A compound leaf with leaflets growing from a common point.

Panicle: A branched and elongated inflorescence of flowers.

Peduncle: The primary (basal) stem of an inflorescence, or the stem bearing a fruit or flower.

Perennial: A plant which will live for three years or more under normal conditions.

Petiole: The primary stalk of a simple or compound leaf. In palm species the stalk beneath the bottom-most leaves or leaflets, and above the leaf sheath or leaf base.

Pinna, pinnae: A leaflet of a pinnate leaf.

Pinnate: Feather-like. A leaf with more than three leaflets growing from the central axis or midrib. The leaflets may grow on opposite sides of the midrib in a single flat plane or they may grow at angles to create a plumose effect.

Pinnatifid: Leaf cut into lobes either side of a central intact region.

Pistil: The female reproductive organ of a flower consisting of the ovary, the style, and the stigma. The ovary is the portion that develops into the fruit. The style is usually a relatively short extension of the ovary, atop which the stigma resides. The stigma receives pollen and stimulates the pollen grains to germinate and grow—by means of a pollen tube—towards the ovules in the ovary. The pollen cell unites with the egg cell in the ovule, which then becomes the embryo of the developing seed.

Pith: Spongy tissue in the center of most stems; the whitish, inner skin of a citrus fruit.

Pyramidal: Crown which is wide at the base, gradually tapering above.

Raceme: An un-branched, elongated, indeterminate inflorescence with pedi-celled flowers.

Rachis: The axis of an inflorescence or of a compound leaf.

Reflexed: Bent sharply backwards.

Rhizome: An underground or above-ground stem growing horizontally and giving rise to roots, stems, and leaves at its nodes or growing tips.

Rib: The primary vein in a leaf.

Rosette: Term applied to a whorl of leaves at the base of the plant.

Seed: Fertilized, ripened ovule, sometimes including the outer layers of a small dry fruit; the dispersed reproductive unit.

Sepal: One of the separate, outermost units of a calyx.

Sessile: Stalkless.

Sheath: The lowest or bottom-most part of a leaf; a widened (often highly so) portion of the bottom of the leaf's petiole where it clasps the stem. Also called leaf base or leaf sheath.

Simple: Leaf not divided into leaflets.

Spathe: Bract-like or petal-like sheath enclosing an inflorescence.

Spathulate: Spoon-shaped; expanded suddenly towards the tip.

Species: The fundamental unit of biological classification, representing a group of closely related individual plants or animals.

Spike: Raceme-like inflorescence with stalkless flowers, as they attach to plant directly.

Spine: A hard, sharp protrusion on a leaf, branch, or stem.

Sprout: Young shoot, sometimes clustered around the base of trunks or from burrs.

Stamens: Pollen producing part of flower with filaments that hold pollen at their tips.

Stigma: The part of the pistil that receives pollen grains and initiates germination.

Stone: Seed enclosed by a hard layer formed from the inner layers of fruit wall.

Sucker: A shoot which arises from an underground shoot or root of a plant.

Succulent: Juicy or fleshy; usually rather thick.

Tap root: A strong root, sometimes swollen, which grows vertically into the soil or compost.

Terminal: At the end or tip, usually of a branch.

Tree: A woody plant with a distinct central trunk.

Umbel: Inflorescence with all the pedicles or penduncles arising from the same point.

Whorled: Leaf form, where three or more leaves radiate from a single node.

Wing: Thin, expanded portion of a seed, fruit or other organ, side petals of a flower of the pea family.

Meanings

Acacia:
Acacia plants are commonly long-lived, and as such are known as gestures of friendship; the longevity of the plant symbolizes the longevity of the relationship. *Acacia* trees are symbols of sensitivity and protection.

Adansonia digitata:
The baobab tree is widely known as the Tree of Life.

Cupressus:
Many cultures consider the cypress to be a very spiritual tree, associated with divine light and heaven.

Eucalyptus:
Traditionally, it is believed that *Eucalyptus* trees have the ability to restore balance to one's life, and to increase vitality.

Ficus:
Ficus trees are symbols of fertility and good fortune. The banyan in particular is known as the World Tree, and is held sacred in many eastern traditions. The peepal tree (*Ficus religiosa*) is a symbol of enlightenment.

Tamarix aphylla:
Athel pines are symbols of protection.

Left
Parkinsonia aculeata
Jerusalem thorn flowers

About the author

Shuaa Abdullah Al-Sada is a former Assistant Professor at Qatar University. During her 18-year career as a member of the Marine Biology Department, Al-Sada collaborated on marine environment research. She received her Bachelor of Science degree from Qatar University, and also holds diplomas in English and French. She developed a love of plants at an early age and remembers her father encouraging her, as a small child, to water and care for fruit trees in their family garden. While travelling, she would often bring back seeds from exotic locations and plant them in her homeland of Qatar. Her amateur fondness of horticulture gradually matured into more academic pursuits; she has done extensive work on a thesis, entitled 'Investigation of the Chemical Ecology of the Red Palm Weevil Rhynchophorus Ferrugineus (Olivier) (Coleoptera: Curculionidea).'

Shuaa Al-Sada has long been concerned about the lack of quality information on plants in her native language, Arabic. She sees this book as a step towards her goal to educate people about the wide variety of plants that can flourish in the Arabian Gulf region. Her dream is to establish an educational farm and garden, to expose both children and adults to the flora of Qatar, and to inspire in them a lifelong love of plants.

Opposite page
Butea monosperma
Flame of the forest flowers

Above
Spathodea campanulata
African tulip tree flowers

About the consultants

Above
Plumeria rubra
Common
frangipani flowers

Sabina Knees has 30 years' experience as a professional botanist, and has held a number of positions with the Royal Horticultural Society, the Royal Botanic Gardens Kew and the Royal Botanic Garden Edinburgh. Her specific interest in Arabian plants, their habitats and conservation stem from her appointment as a research botanist on the Flora of the Arabian Peninsula and Socotra at the Royal Botanic Garden Edinburgh in 2005. She is now a research associate at the Centre for Middle Eastern Plants, part of RBGE.

Sabina currently focuses on all aspects of the Flora of the Arabian Peninsula and Socotra, including IUCN conservation assessments of Arabian taxa through membership of Species Survival Commission Plant Specialist Groups, and running field training courses. Her extensive fieldwork experience has concentrated on the Gulf States, Oman and Yemen, and a significant amount of her time has been spent in an advisory role with the Oman Botanic Garden. Sabina has supervised several PhD, MSc and undergraduate research students from various countries in the region, on a wide range of subjects relating to Middle Eastern plant taxonomy, evolution and conservation.

Lorna MacKinnon has over 10 years' experience in plant taxonomy, including roles with the Centre for Middle Eastern Plants at the Royal Botanic Garden Edinburgh, Oman Botanic Garden and the Eden Project in Cornwall, UK. Her interest in Arabian plants started with her appointment as assistant seed bank curator and field taxonomist with Oman Botanic Garden in 2010, and continued with contributions to the Flora of the Arabian Peninsula and Socotra including accounts of the Juncaceae and Cyperaceae.

Lorna has had a broad range of fieldwork experience, particularly in the arid regions of Oman, the UAE, Libya and Jordan, and also in Cameroon, California and Henderson Island. She currently holds the position of plant records officer with the Eden Project, managing the database of the living plant collection.

Above
Bauhinia variegata
Orchid tree flower

Right
Cocos nucifera
Coconut palms